much because she
pioneered classical
music into Christian
education in Arkansas.

In Jesus,
Willodine Hopkins

SIGNIFICANT WOMEN IN THE SIGNS OF GOD

Willodine Hopkins and
Nita Brinkley-Smith

AuthorHouse™
1663 Liberty Drive
Bloomington, IN 47403
www.authorhouse.com
Phone: 1-800-839-8640

First published by AuthorHouse 2/23/2010

ISBN: 978-1-4490-7094-6 (e)
ISBN: 978-1-4490-7095-3 (sc)

Printed in the United States of America
Bloomington, Indiana

This book is printed on acid-free paper.

Grateful acknowledgment to Roy Seay for proofreading this book. A special thanks to Paula and Roy Seay for technical assistance on the computer.
Cover design by Roy Seay--Photographs from Roy Seay's archives

This book is dedicated to:

The Seay Sisters:
Marge Murray
Tilda O'Neal
Anna Lewis
Nancy Gammill
Betty Foster
Shiela Mullins

CONTENTS

Lesson 1…Eve… A Snake…1
Sign Significance…Sin Causes Spiritual Death

Lesson 2…Noah's wife… Rainbow…13
Sign significance…God Keeps HIS promises

Lesson 3…Sarah…Laughter…25
Sign Significance… God Gives Joy To HIS People

Lesson 4…Hagar…Visited by An Angel Twice…39
Sign Significance…God Sees Our Struggles

Lesson 5…Jochebed…. Unafraid…51
Sign significance…. In The Shadows Of Idols,
Taught Her Son About God

Lesson 6…Miriam…Got Leprosy Because She Was
Racially Prejudiced…63
Sign Significance…God Will Not Let Racial
Prejudice Go Unpunished

Lesson 7…Hannah…Could Not See God Working
In Her Life 73
Sign Significance…Do Not Judge…
(Only God Knows What He Is Doing In A Life)

Lesson 8… Huldah…Knew Word Of God From
False Prophet's Message 85
Sign Significance…Christians Can Distinguish
The Real Word Of God From Fake Messages

Lesson 9…Mary, The Virgin Mother Of Jesus 95
Sign Significance…Jesus Is Truly The Son Of God

Lesson 10…Mary Magdalene…Gratefully Cared
For Jesus And His Disciples..109
Sign significance…Role Model For Christian Women

Lesson 11…Pilate's Wife…Warned Her Husband
Not To Harm Jesus..121
Sign Significance…Do No Harm To Jesus

Lesson 12…Chosen Lady In The Book Of II John.......................133
Sign Significance…The Church Is The Bride Of Christ

Part II

Unknown Women Whose Good Influence In Today's World Make It A Better Planet

Chapter 13 Marge L. Murray...150

Chapter 14 Tilda O'Neal..153

Chapter 15 Anna Lewis 157

Chapter 16 Nancy Gammill....161

Chapter 17 Betty Louise Foster....165

Chapter 18 Sheila Ann Mullins....169

Chapter 19 Linda McGarraugh Hoppe....173

Chapter 20 Lorene Nichols Leath....177

Chapter 21 Ellen Dolores Jones Bristoe....181

Chapter 22 Celia Solis Boon....185

Chapter 23 Mary Stobaugh Shambarger....189

Chapter 24 Susan Shambarger Goss....195

Chapter 25 Deborah (Deb) Sue Williams Kee....199

Chapter 26 Brenda Hines Myers....203

Chapter 27 Georgia Faye Howell Cook....209

Chapter 28 Tserenpel Tsendja....215

Chapter 29 Ruby Louise Shaver Wilson....221

This Time In History

Vic Underwood

When my family celebrated my seventy-fifth birthday, I met an outstanding couple, Vic and Janet Underwood. Vic's vocation is in Transportation in Trucking Sales. He and Janet have seven children and four grandchildren.

Vic shared with me an essay he had written about This Time In History. I asked him if I could print it in this book because it is so thought provoking. He readily agreed. I know that you will enjoy reading it. Willodine Hopkins

The mystery of this time in history is that we have taller buildings, but shorter tempers, wider freeways, but narrower insight. We spend more, but have less; we buy more, but enjoy less. We have bigger houses and smaller families, more conveniences, but less time to serve others. We have more degrees, but less common sense, more knowledge, but less judgment, more experts, yet more problems, more medicine, but fewer healthy people.

We drink too much, play on the computer too much, spend time too recklessly, laugh too little, drive too fast, get too angry, stay up too late, get up too tired, read too little, watch television too much, pray too seldom and meditate on Scripture too little.

We have multiplied our possessions, but reduced our values. We talk too much, listen too little, love too seldom, and hate too often.

We may have learned how to make a living, but not a blessed life. We've added years to life not life to years. We've been all the way to the moon and back, but have trouble crossing the street to meet or help our neighbor. We conquered outer space but not our inner greatness of His power toward us who believe. We've done larger things, but not better things.

We've cleaned up the air, but polluted the soul. We've conquered the atom, but not our prejudice toward folks that are not quite like us. We write more, but learn less. We plan more, but accomplish less. We've learned to rush, but not to wait. We build more computers to hold more information, to produce more copies than ever, but we communicate less and less.

These are the times of fast foods and slow digestion, big strong athletes and small character, steep profits and shallow or no relationships. These are the days of two incomes, but more divorce, fancier houses, but broken homes. These are the days of quick trips, disposable diapers, throwaway morality, one night stands, overweight bodies, and pills that do everything from cheer, to quiet, to kill. It is a time when there is a lot of glitter in the showroom window and nothing in the *love, joy, peace, patience, kindness, goodness, faithfulness,* and *self-control* stockroom.

Remember to spend time with your loved ones, because they are not going to be around forever.

Remember to say a kind word to someone who looks up to you in awe, because that little person will soon grow up and leave your side.

Remember to give a warm hug to your family and close friends, because this is the treasure you can give with your heart and it does not cost a cent.

Remember to say, "I love you" to your family, but most of all mean it. A kiss and an embrace will mend a hurt when it comes from God and not your own fleshly desires.

Remember to hold hands and cherish the moment for someday your child will be gone.

Give time to love, give time to speak! Give time to share the precious thoughts of your mind.

And always remember:

Life is not measured by the number of breaths we take,
but the moments that take our breath away.

CHAPTER 1

SIGNIFICANT WOMAN...EVE

Significant Sign...The Serpent Deceived Her

Now the serpent was more crafty than any of the wild animals the LORD God had made He said to the woman, "Did God really say, 'You must not eat from any tree in the garden'?"

The woman said to the serpent, "We may eat fruit from the trees in the garden, but God did say, "You must not eat from the tree that is in the middle of the garden, and you must not touch it, or you will die.

"You will not surely die," the serpent said to the woman. For God knows that when you eat of it your eyes will be opened, and you will be like God, knowing good and evil."

(Genesis 3:1-5)

Most people in the Christian world are acquainted with the story of Adam, Eve, and the serpent in the Garden of Eden. Nearly every Bible commentary states that Adam was with Eve when the serpent tempted her. Adam did not try to deter her from eating the forbidden fruit, and he willingly ate it when she offered it to him.

God cursed all three, Adam, Eve, and the serpent. Every woman who suffers agony in childbirth suffers because of the curse as a result of Eve's listening to the crafty serpent's beguiling words. Any woman who strives to please God sometimes rankles under being in submission to her husband; this is also part of Eve's curse.

Analyses of these verses suggest that pain in childbirth is the curse for Eve's first sin. Sin is so terrible and repugnant to God that every woman since Eve, who has had a baby, suffers almost unbearable agony because of Eve's only one sin. It is difficult for us humans to see sin as God sees sin.

When God placed the blame for the first sins, HE cursed the serpent first. The Bible does not specifically state it, but all Bible scholars believe that satan entered the body of the serpent causing it to be crafty.

"Because you have done this,
"Cursed are you above all livestock
and all of the wild animals!
You will crawl on your belly
and you will eat dust
all of the days of your life."
(Genesis 3:14)

Snake skeletons have leg sockets in them, but no leg bones. It would be interesting to know how the snake looked, long and thin as they are, walking on four legs. Of greater interest would be, did the animals loose their ability to talk with mankind because of Adam's and Eve's sins? History records that Solomon could communicate with the animals; that was part of his God-given wisdom. Solomon understood the animal's communications systems. The animals did not come up to everyone and make casual conversation in their own language as the serpent did when it talked to Eve.

After God cursed Adam, Eve, and the serpent, HE showed HIS mercy by giving Adam and Eve hope that their sin would be forgiven and not held against them. God said:

"And I will put enmity
between you and the woman,
and between your offspring and hers ,
He will crush your head
and you will strike his heel."
(Genesis 3:15-16)

Jesus crushed the head of satan when HE led a sinless life, died on the cross, was raised from the dead and established HIS kingdom on earth. Because Jesus lives in Christians; when a Christian sins, it hurts HIM by symbolically striking HIS heel. This is seen when HE appeared to Saul of Tarsus the first time and telling Saul that his persecuting the new Christians in HIS kingdom hurt HIM (Acts 26:14).

***

Dan, A "Serpent By The Roadside"

Dan will provide justice for his people
as one of the tribes of Israel.
Dan will be a serpent by the roadside,
a viper along the path
that bites the horses' heels
so that the rider tumbles backward

I look for your deliverance, O LORD.
(Genesis 49:16-17)

When Jacob gave his blessings and prophesies about his twelve sons, it's as if when he got to Dan, he said, "I have good news and bad news." Dan will provide justice for his people and he will be a serpent along the path causing travelers to have trouble on the road. The Bible says about God's throne, "*Righteousness and justice are the foundation of your throne; love and faithfulness go before you* (Psalm 89:14).

Dan was the son of Bilhah, Rachel's handmaid. Dan grew up seeing his father Jacob being partial to Joseph and Benjamin. He, along with his other brothers, resented such favoritism. As Jacob was dying and telling his sons what God had shown him to say about their futures, it seems as if Jacob looked back over his life and could see the injustice done to his sons and especially Dan. His plaintive cry, "I look for your deliverance O LORD," goes in two directions. Jacob was looking back at the environment in which his sons were reared and the great event of God's Son coming to earth to deliver people from their sins.

For many years the serpent was put on the flag of the tribe of Dan. But Jewish folklore says that one day Ahiezer, descendant of Dan, saw an eagle kill a snake. He had the serpent removed from their tribe's flag and had the eagle embroidered on it instead. He believed that God meant for the evil snake to be removed from his tribe's flag. He wanted to inspire his people to fulfill the prophecy by providing justice, not be like the crafty snakes.

About 700 BC many of the tribe of Dan migrated to Europe. They founded Denmark; Den meaning Dan. Their tracks can be traced all across Europe. The Danube River, Dunkirk in England, and especially in Ireland. The name Dun or Dunn means justice. Ruling kings and queens sometimes married spouses from the tribe of Dan in order to show their subjects that justice would be done under their rule. Then they had eagles embroidered on their flags. The eagles, symbolizing justice, found its way into the United States. Our founding fathers wanted it known that in this country liberty and justice would be provided for all.

***

The Brazen Serpent In The Wilderness

When the Canaanite king of Arad, who lived in the Negev, heard that Israel was coming along the road to Atharim, he attacked the Israelites and captured some of them. Then Israel made this vow to the LORD: "If you will deliver these people into our hands, we will totally destroy their cities. The LORD listened to Israel's plea and gave the Canaanites over to them. They completely destroyed them and their towns, so the place was named Hormah.

They traveled from Mount Hor along the road to the Red Sea, to go around Edom. But the people grew impatient on the way; they spoke against God and against Moses, and said, "Why have you brought us up out of Egypt to die in the desert? There is no bread! There is no water! And we detest this miserable food!"

Then the LORD sent venomous snakes among them; they bit the people and many Israelites died. The people came to Moses and said, "We sinned when we spoke against the LORD and against you. Pray that the LORD will take the snakes away from us. So Moses prayed for the people.

The LORD said to Moses, "Make a snake and put it on a pole; anyone who is bitten can look at it and live." So Moses made a bronze snake and put it on a pole. Then when anyone was bitten by a snake and looked on the bronze snake, he lived.

(Numbers 21: 1-9)

Before we judge the ancient Israelites who were victorious over their enemies and before the victory celebration had ended began complaining to God about their life situation; we need to look at our own hearts and see if we have behaved in the same way. Every Christian has been delivered from sin, and while we are still rejoicing over how God delivered us, we complain our taxes are too much, our homes are too small, our vehicle is not new, we do not have elite friends, etc. Does God get angry with us because of our complaining? Yes HE does!

What incredible symbolism in this passage of Scripture. God delivers their enemies into their hands mightily. Yet, there is no record of the Israelites being grateful in their hearts and giving any public display of their gratitude for their deliverance. Instead of gratitude, they began to grumble and complain over their situation in life. People have not changed.

When God disciplines us for our ingratitude and complaining, HE knows exactly what it takes to get us into prayer. It may be as bitter an experience as the fiery serpents that bit the Israelites and even killed many of them. As the Israelites were told to look upon the brazen serpent on the pole, so Christians are commanded to look upon Christ on the cross.

It is doubtful if anyone who looked upon the serpent on the pole knew that it was a sign of Jesus, the Son of God, being nailed upon a cross for all the sins ever committed by any one who ever lived in this world. It foreshadowed their Savior. On the cross Jesus would deeply wound satan's head, and satan would wound Jesus' heel. Even Christians today would probably have a difficult time seeing the connection, had not Jesus said HIMSELF, "*Just as Moses lifted up the snake in the desert, so the Son of man must be lifted up, that everyone who believes in him may have eternal life*" ((John 3:14-14). HE also said, "*Now is the time for judgment on this world; now the prince of this world will be driven out. But when I am lifted up from the earth, will draw all men to myself.*"

Those who do not lift up Christ in their lives and tell all the world about Jesus will suffer the wrathful judgment of God They will suffer eternally with satan, who is represented by the snake. Christ led a perfect life when HE lived upon this earth, but when HE died on the cross, HE bore every sin that anyone has ever done or will do. Being laden with our sins, he became, symbolically speaking, the evil snake.

***

Hezekiah Destroyed The Brazen Serpent Many In Today's World Still Worship It

*He (*Hezekiah*) did what was right in the eyes of the LORD, just as his father David had done. He removed the high places, smashed the bronze snake Moses had made, for up to that time the Israelites had been burning incense to it. (It was called Nehushtan.* (II Kings 18:4)

The succeeding generations of Israelites who lived after Moses died, saw only faintly, if they saw any sign at all, that the serpent was a sign connected with a future Savior. God used the serpent as a sign that all evil sins would be nailed on the cross. In their shallow understanding of the sign, they began to worship the serpent that was a sign of sins against God. As King Hezekiah went about doing what was right in God's sight, he destroyed the serpent because his subjects had made it an object of worship and were not obeying the first and second of the Ten Commandments.

As Israel was on the Silk Road that connected Egypt and the other African counties to the rest of the world, many visitors traveling through Israel saw the Jews worshipping the serpent, Nehushtan, and they began to worship it as a god also.

The worship of Nehushtan continued through the many centuries and many people today worship the serpent god Nehushtan. The surname of many persons living in the world today is Nehushtan. They are not to be connected with the bronze serpent that Moses made in the wilderness anymore than the surname Cain, Kane, or Kaine bears any connection with Biblical Cain who killed his brother.

Wisdom is connected with their worship of serpents. It is not true wisdom because it is connected with worshipping a symbol of evil. They claim their serpent god has founded great and advanced civilizations in South America, China, India, and many other smaller countries; and has a longer history that the history of worshipping Jesus. Some claim their god's history goes back to baal. Any form of serpent worship is a form of satan worship and should be completely avoided by Christians.

Paul And The Serpent On Malta

Once safely on shore, we found out that the island was called Malta. The islanders showed us unusual kindness. They built a fire and welcomed us because it was raining and cold. Paul gathered a pile of brushwood and as he put it on the fire, a viper was driven out by the heat, fastened itself on his hand. When the islanders saw the snake hanging from his hand, they said to each other, "This man must be a murderer; for though he escaped from the sea, Justice has not allowed him to live." But Paul shook the snake off into the fire and suffered no ill effects. The people expected him to swell up or suddenly fall dead, but after waiting a long time and seeing nothing unusual happen to him, they changed their minds and said he was a god.

(Acts 28:1-5)

He (Jesus) said to them, "Go into all of the world and preach the good news to all creation. Whoever believes and is baptized will be saved, but whoever does not believe will be condemned. And all of these signs will accompany all of those who believe: In my name they will drive out demons, they will speak in new tongues, <u>they will pick up snakes with their hands;</u> and when they drink a deadly poison, it will not hurt them at all, they will place their hands on sick people and they will get well."

(Mark 16:15-18)

Paul did not go out and find a snake to handle to show the power God had given to him as an apostle. The snake was already in the sticks that Paul picked up to help keep the fire going so that all could get warm. They were chilled from being in the cold water and needed the warmth. God did not allow Paul to be harmed by the bite. Since Paul was HIS apostle and was given special powers in order to show others that Jesus is truly the Savior of the world.

Paul, the apostle, and all apostles were given special powers to prove to the people to whom they were preaching that they were indeed telling the true Word of God. They also had the authority to transfer their miraculous powers to whomever the Holy Spirit chose by laying their hands upon that chosen one. Today we have the Word of God in written form: The Bible. Many miraculous signs done by the apostles and others upon whom the apostles laid their hands confirmed it as the true Word of God. *This salvation, which was first announced by the Lord, was confirmed to us by those who heard him. God also testified to it by signs, wonders and various miracles, and gifts of the Holy Spirit distributed according to His will* (Hebrews 2: 3b-4).

***

The Serpent Looses The Battle

And there was war in heaven. Michael and his angels fought against the dragon, and the dragon and his angels fought back. But he (the dragon) was not strong enough, and they lost their place in heaven. The great dragon was hurled down...that ancient serpent called the devil or satan, who leads the whole world astray. He was hurled to the earth, and his angels with him.

Then I heard a voice in heaven say:

Now have come the salvation and the power and the
Kingdom of our God,
and the authority of his Christ.
For the accuser of our brothers,
who accuses them before God day and night,
has been hurled down.
They overcame him
by the blood of the Lamb,
and by the word of their testimony;
they did not love their lives so much
as to shrink from death.
Therefore rejoice, you heavens
and you who dwell in them!
But woe to the earth and to the sea,
Because the devil has gone down to you!
He is filled with fury
Because he knows that his time is short.
(Revelation 12:7-12)

Our battle against satan is not over. He was thrown out of heaven where Christians are going when life as we know it on this earth will be over. He will be cast into eternal hell along with those who are not children of God. The text states that Christians overcome satan by:

(1)...the blood of the Lamb (Jesus)

(2)...by the word of their testimony

(3)...and not loving our lives so much as to shrink back from death

We Christians must be aggressively busy telling others about Jesus and learning to hate our own lives enough to give them up for the cause of Christ.

Notes

Chapter 1 Small Groups Discussion Questions

Break into groups of three to five people.
Each group will discuss one study question.
One spokesperson will report to the class the group's discussion of the question assigned to them.

1. Every woman, including Eve, has had to suffer in childbearing, as a consequence for only one sin, discuss how much God hates sin.

2. The Bible does not say when satan entered into the serpent in the Garden of Eden, how do we know it was really the devil that lied to Eve and tempted her to sin?

3. The generation died that had looked upon the brazen serpent in the wilderness and got well, but at some point in time they will learn or have learned that the serpent represented Jesus who bore all of our sins. Discuss what it will be like in heaven to meet some of them and talk about how you read their story in the Bible. How do you think they will react to meeting you?

4. Hezekiah destroyed the brazen serpent because people were worshipping it instead of God. Discuss why your group thinks why they did this.

5. How do we talk with sincere people who handle snakes in their worship service to let them learn the Bible does not teach this as an act of worship?

CHAPTER 2

SIGNIFICANT WOMAN... NOAH'S WIFE

Significant Sign...Rainbow, The Promise Of Hope

Any people who have read some of the Bible or watched television know the story of Noah and the Ark. It captures the imagination because of its scope and drama.

The LORD saw how great man's wickedness on the earth had become, that every inclination of the thoughts of his heart was only evil all of the time. The LORD was grieved that he had made man on the earth, and his heart was filled with pain. So the LORD said, "I will wipe mankind, whom I have created, from the face of the earth---men and animals, and creatures that move along the ground, and birds in the air--for I am grieved that I have made them. But Noah found grace in the eyes of the LORD.

(Genesis 6:5-8)

God's heart was filled with pain, not because HE behaves like a petulant two-year-old who has his after dinner candy taken from him because he did not eat his vegetables. God is all-knowing. HE knows the reality of what sin is. HE knows the pain of having to turn HIS face from HIS beloved creation because HE will not allow HIMSELF to look upon sin. HE is completely pure, completely wise, and completely righteous.

***

Who was Mrs. Noah?

*The Scriptures do not tell us Noah's wife name, but ancient Jewish folklore remembers her name was Naamah, the daughter of Enoch, who did not die, but was taken into heaven. One of her brothers was Methuselah, who was not a great follower of God, but was taught about God the same as Naamah. She was Noah's great aunt.

Genealogy chart

Enoch (seventh generation from Adam)
|
Methuselah (son)… Namaah (daughter)
|
Lamech (son)
|
Noah (son)

Before Naamah's father was taken into heaven, he arranged for her to marry Noah, the only man on earth Enoch could find who was a worshipper of the true God. While others were having lavish weddings with idols set around and being paid obeisance by having sex orgies and debauchery; Namaah's wedding honored only the True God, the Holy Creator.

There was no 'honeymoon baby' the next year. Noah was five hundred years old before they had their first son. If we assume that they were married about the time that Noah was twenty years old:

Marriage...20 years old
<...480 years pass...>
500 years old ...Shem, Ham and Japheth born

***

Naamah and Noah Had Four-Hundred-Eighty Years Of Trials

1... **No children**

How many, many times they were rudely encouraged to visit the temple of idols, and ask advice as to what to do to have children. "You worship an unseen God. Your God does not exist; you need to worship a god that is seen. Worship Ianna, the fertility goddess and then you will have no problem having a large family."

2.... Not socially prominent

Her brother Methuselah and his family were invited to 'every social event', but they did not invite Naamah and her husband, Noah. Naamah dressed differently (modestly) and they ate differently; they never ate food offered to idols. "They are out-of-touch with what's going on, non-intellectual and condemning us, they are pains-in-the-neck. They are so ignorant they call our worship fornication and adultery! Don't ever invite them to anything!!"

3...Their speech was unacceptable

Their neighbors complained to the civil authorities, "They never invoke the names of our many gods... when they hear us, they quickly tell us that there is only one true God. HIS name is to be held in great reverence because HIS Name is too holy to say lightly.

4... 525,600 lonely mealtimes

Naamah cooked about 1,095 meals per year for 480 years, making 525,600 meals which most of the time there were only two at the table. No one wanted to visit or eat with Naamah and Noah because they worshipped only one unseen God. Naamah carefully selected their food and bought only what was not offered to idols. She had to pay high prices because they were social outcasts. Gourmet foods were unavailable to them.

5...24,960 miserable wash days

Washdays were not miserable because Namaah did not like to do laundry. They were sore trials because she had to endure being demeaned by the town's women because of her disgrace of not having any children. Their laundry loads were much larger than Namaah had to carry. They talked of morning sickness and having babies. They spoke of their babies having colic and losing sleep in ways that told Namaah they were happy to loose sleep because their husbands and the townspeople held them in honor. If only Namaah would seek and take the advice of the local idolatrous priests, she could have children, too. Someone usually said, "Do you enjoy living in such dishonor, Namaah?"

After Noah was 500 years old,
he became the father of Shem, Ham, and Japheth.
(Genesis 5:32)

***

God Commanded Noah To Build An Ark

God told Noah it was going to rain and flood the entire earth. Namaah's husband took on two new vocations, "Preacher of Righteousness" and "Boat Builder. He preached that water was going to fall from the sky and flood the entire earth. "Water falling from the sky," he said," is called rain." Their neighbors laughed at them and said scornfully, "It has never rained on this earth before and we do not believe you!" He preached that all who did not worship and obey the only true God were going to drown in the water that would cover the earth. Things looked strange around Noah's house because Noah began collecting two of every animal to take on the ark.

For about one-hundred-twenty years Noah preached and built the ark. Namaah's sons helped their father. They grew up and married (There is no consensus in ancient history as to the exact names of their wives'). The day came when God said to put the animals inside the ark, after they were all placed snugly inside, they boarded and God shut the door.

They were inside the ark one full week before it began to rain. The Bible does not state what they did for that week, but it can be surmised that it was a week of neighbors beating on the door, and begging them to come out into the real world. They probably told Naamah and Noah that they were insane.

Their faith was tested as severely, as if by fire for seven long days.. God told then to go inside the ark and HE shut the door. Neighbors knew why they were inside the ark, Noah and Naamah believed water was going to fall from heaven. The neighbors knew what Noah preached, but not one drop of rain fell from the sky. This trial was far more trying than the one-hundred-twenty years it took to build the ark and gather all of the animals, because nothing happened!!!

After the long week ended horrendous lightning began to flash and deafening thunder began to roar. Then it began to rain, something that had never happened on the earth before. Their faith became reality. God had commanded and they had obeyed. It rained constantly for forty days and forty nights and killed every creature on the earth that breathed air.

After the rain ceased, it was another three-hundred-forty days before the waters went down enough for them to put heir feet on the ground. They stayed inside the ark for a total of three-hundred-seventy days; five days over a year the way we count time today.

***

The First Rainbow

Then God said to Noah, "Come out of the ark, you and your wife and your sons and their wives. Bring out every kind of living creature that is with you, the birds, the animals, and all of the creatures that move along the ground---so they can multiply on the earth and be fruitful and increase in number upon it."

(Genesis 8:15-16)

When they disembarked they saw the first rainbow ever on earth. They marveled at its seven colors, red, orange, yellow, green, blue, indigo, and violet. How beautiful! God promised that never again would HE destroy the earth by water and gave the sign of the rainbow to remind them. God said:

" As long as the earth endures,
seedtime and harvest,
cold and heat,
summer and winter,
day and night,
will never cease."
(Genesis 8:22)

Bible scholars have written much explaining when God uses the number seven, HE means completeness. A partial list of the sevens in the human body is:

Human Eye...seven colors
Human Voice...seven tones
Human Nose...seven basic scents
Human Tongue...seven basic taste areas
Human head...seven orifices
(Two eyes, two ears, two nostrils, and one mouth)

***

The New Law

God also gave the survivors of the flood a new law:

"Be fruitful and increase in number and fill the earth. The fear and dread of you will fall upon all beasts of the earth and all of the birds of the air, upon every creature that moves upon the ground, and upon all of the fish of the sea; they are given into you hands. Everything that moves will be food for you. Just as I gave you green plants, I now give you everything.

But you must not eat meat that has its lifeblood in it. And for your lifeblood I will surely demand an accounting. I will demand an accounting from every animal. And from each man, too I will demand accounting for the life of his fellow man.

"Whoever sheds the blood of man,
by man shall his blood be shed;
for in the image of God
has God made man.

As for you be fruitful and increase in number, multiply on the earth and increase upon it. (Genesis 9:1-7)

A careful reading of the text reveals that mankind was vegetarian until the flood. God, in the new world after the flood, gave people meat to eat. It must have been an exciting experience for Naamah to prepare roasted meat. What animal did she cook first? The Bible does not say. How strange they all felt when they put meat in their mouths for the first time. They realized that everyone they knew in their former life did not know how meat tasted. No one rebelled against God concerning HIS new law by saying, "We've never done this before." They were people of faith…everyone began to eat meat.

***

The New Sign, The Rainbow

Then God said to Noah and his sons with him. "I now establish my covenant with you and your descendants after you and with every living creature that was with you---the birds, the livestock, and all of the wild animals, all those that came out of the ark with you---every living creature on earth. I will establish my covenant with you:

Never again will all life be cut off by the waters of a flood; never again will there be a flood to destroy the earth."

And God said, "This is the sign of the covenant I am making between me and you and every living creature with you, a covenant for all generations to come. I have set my rainbow in the clouds, and it will be a sign of the covenant between me and earth. Whenever I bring clouds over the earth, and the rainbow appears in the clouds, I will remember my covenant between me and you and all living creatures of every kind. Never again will the waters become a flood to destroy all life. Whenever a rainbow appears in the clouds, I will see it and remember the everlasting covenant between God and all living creatures of every kind on the earth."

So God said to Noah, "This is the sign of the covenant I have established between me and all of the earth."

(Genesis 8:8-17)

Whenever Christians see a rainbow today, their hearts thrill because they remember the covenant God made with humans and animals after the flood. What an animal knows is a great mystery to humans. Zoologists are busy today working with chimpanzees, dolphins and many other animals. They wish to discover the scope of how much animals know. Your author would like to know if animals know the meaning of the sign of the rainbow, since God made the covenant between HIMSELF, man and animals.

***

God's Character

God keeps HIS promises! Since God promised so long ago that seedtime and harvest, cold and heat, summer and winter, day and night will never cease, HE is still keeping these promises today. The sun rose today giving us in the western hemisphere light, while the eastern hemisphere has night. Our northern hemisphere has spring while the southern hemisphere has autumn. Day and night never cease on the earth. Summer and winter never cease on the earth. God keeps HIS promises!

His divine power has given us everything we need for life and godliness through our knowledge of him who called us by his own glory and goodness. Through these he has given us his very great and precious promises, so that we may participate in the divine nature and escape the corruption in the world caused by evil desires.

(II Peter 1:3-4)

Because we can see the rainbow, the sign that there will never be another global flood, and observe that day and night or seasons have never ceased; by faith we can know that every exceedingly great and precious promise HE has promised us will come to pass.

In our faith walk we may be:

1…Beginning to build an ark, or
2…Rounding up animals to put inside the ark, or
3…Putting the finishing touches on an ark, or
4…Sitting inside the ark for seven dry days,
…while The world outside the ark is persecuting us for our faith.
…Our friends turn away from us,
…and our jobs and sometimes our lives are in jeopardy,
…but all is well
…because,
…we continually study and obey the Word of God,
…we are safe in a covenant relationship with HIM,
…when
…the storm is over,
…we get off the ark and see,
…God's rainbow sign assuring us that HE keeps HIS promises.
…We bow and pray giving thanks to HIM, who will keep us in HIS arms now and for all eternity.

***

Notes

Chapter 2 Small Groups Discussion Questions

Break into groups of three to five people.
Each group will discuss one study question.
One spokesperson will report to the class the group's discussion of the question assigned to them.

1. More people in the world who know anything about the Old Testament know the story of the flood and the rainbow than any other story. Do you think God planned it that way? There are no wrong answers.

2. Noah married Enoch's daughter. Enoch walked with God and never had to die, God took him to be with HIM. Can you see God's providential hand in choosing a wife for Noah? Tell events in your own lives where you see God's hand moving in your own life.

3. Noah built the ark exactly according to the pattern God told him. If he had changed the pattern, the ark may not have made it safely through the storm. Why is it so important that people today follow exactly the pattern God has given us for our lives?

4. Discuss the traumas Naamah suffered before she had Shem, Ham, and Japheth.

5. What does the rainbow mean to you today? Be specific in your answers.

CHAPTER 3

SIGNIFICANT WOMAN...SARAH

Significant Sign...Laughter, God Made Her Laugh

God also said to Abraham, "As for Sarai your wife, you are no longer to call her Sarai; her name will be Sarah. I will bless her and she will be the mother of nations; kings of people will come from her."

Abraham fell face down; he laughed and said to himself, "Will a son be born to a man a hundred years old? Will Sarah bear a child at the age of ninety? And Abraham said to God, If only Ishmael might live under your blessing?

Then God said, "Yes, but your wife Sarah will bear you a son and you will call him Isaac. I will establish my covenant with him as an everlasting covenant for his descendants after him.

(Genesis17:15-19)

God announced to Abraham that he and Sarah would have a son. Abraham laughed, a reaction to his disbelief because of the human impossibility of what was told to him. Later God repeated to Abraham the same unbelievable news:

"Where is your wife Sarah?" they asked him.
"There in the tent," he (Abraham) said.
Then the LORD said, "I will surely return to you
about this time next year,
and Sarah your wife will have a son.

Now Sarah was listening at the entrance to the tent, which was behind him. Abraham and Sarah were already old and well advanced in years, and Sarah was past the age of childbearing. So Sarah laughed to herself as she thought, "After I am worn out and my master is old, will I now have this pleasure?"

Then the LORD said to Abraham, "Why did Sarah laugh and say, 'Will I really have a child, now that I am old?'

Is anything too hard for the LORD?

I will return to you at the appointed time next year and Sarah will have a son."

Sarah was afraid, so she lied and said," I did not laugh."
But he (the LORD) said, "Yes, you did laugh."
(Genesis 18:10-15)

Sarah laughed with the same disbelief of the impossibility of her ever getting pregnant as old as she was. Yet, the impossible happened! At the appointed time Isaac was born exactly as the LORD had promised. Many read about Sarah becoming pregnant, and conclude that the LORD restored Sarah's youth including making her ovaries and womb viable. Her breasts were able to produce milk for her newborn son. In her youth, Sarah was a legendary beauty. God did not restore Abraham's youth; because many men, and Abraham was one like these, do not loose their ability to make viable sperm and to have sex in their old age. He showed this was possible because Hagar became pregnant after one sexual encounter with Abraham.

After Isaac was born:

Sarah said, God has brought me to laughter,
and everyone who hears about this will laugh with me."
And she added,
"Who would have said to Abraham that Sarah would nurse children? Yet I have born him a son in his old age."
(Genesis 21: 6-7)

Sarah had endured Hagar's scornful laughter after Hagar became pregnant with Ishmael and for thirteen years, because Hagar had youth and beauty and fertility. When Sarah thought about it she admitted she deserved it. Because it was she who thought up the plan to use Hagar instead of believing Abraham when he told her God promised him a son (Genesis: Chapter16).

Read carefully her words, "*Yet I have born him a son in his old age.*" It can be inferred: She was no longer an old barren woman, but a woman who could nurse a child at her breasts and she is, in a sense, laughing about the fact that she was young, beautiful and fertile. God had made her to laugh with true joy in HIM. Abraham also laughed with joy because God's promise to him had been fulfilled.

***

Mrs. Job, Who Scorned Her Husband

On another day the angels came to present themselves before the LORD, and satan came with them to present himself before him. And the LORD said to satan, "Where have you come from?"

Satan answered the LORD, "From roaming through the earth and going back and forth in it."

Then the LORD said to satan, "Have you considered my servant Job. There is no one on earth like him; he is blameless and upright, a man who fears God and shuns evil. And he still maintains his integrity though you incited me against him to ruin him without any reason."

"Skin for skin!" satan replied. A man will give all he has for his own life. But stretch out your hand and strike his flesh and bones and he will surely curse you to your face."

The LORD said to satan, "Very well then, he is in your hands, but you must spare his life."

So satan went out from the presence of the LORD and afflicted Job with painful sores from the soles of his feet to the top of his head. Then Job took a piece of broken pottery and scraped himself with it as he sat among the ashes.

His wife said to him, "Are you still holding to your integrity? Curse God and die!"

He replied, "You are talking like a foolish woman. Shall we accept good from God and not trouble? In all this Job did not sin in what he said

(Job 2: 1-10)

Her husband was the richest man in the country. A beautiful palace-like home was hers to enjoy and she was one of the best-dressed women in the country. All of her children were successful in business and happy. When she went out in public, everyone knew who she was and respected her.

In a short period of time her life changed drastically. All of her children were dead. Her grief was inconsolable. The beautiful home and all of the money she could ever want were gone. Job, her husband was eaten alive with sores and he could not provide her with enough to eat.

She had no career training, so she had to hire out and do menial work for mere pennies that were not enough to buy food to fill both their stomachs. Some ancient manuscripts say she sold her luxurious hair to buy food. All she ever saw Job do was to moan and try to seek relief from his pain by scraping his sores with broken bits of pottery, but he never blamed God. God, in her mind, was the cause of all of their troubles, they had done nothing to deserve this kind of treatment from HIM.

One can almost hear her scornful laughter when she asked him, "Are you still holding on to your integrity?" Job believed to keep one's integrity was to recognize God as the one who makes one whole. He considered himself whole in God's eyes even though he was poor, grief-stricken and racked with painful sores.

To her, Job may have been a 'whole' man, but he was not the man she married and had lived with and had ten children. In her mind it was better to sacrifice one's integrity and have the comforts of life w than to be the wife of a 'whole' man who was so sick that she had to work and beg for their living.

If Job were dead, she could clean herself up and attract a new husband, who could provide her with a respectable living. Maybe she would not be the richest woman in the country, but she certainly would not be the wife of a man who was the poorest and sickest in the country. Other men she knew did not talk about God much of their time and did not feel compelled to thank HIM in all of their circumstances.

She vented her inner feelings and said, "Curse God and die!" She really believed that Job would die if he cursed God. Her faith was not great enough to be God's woman in all circumstances of her life. But her true belief was that God would take Job's life if he cursed HIM and then she would be free to pursue a life free of him. It is extremely doubtful that Mrs. Job would ever do as she requested Job to do. She wanted him to die and she was not ready to die.

Perhaps she was like many Christians today. They attend church services regularly, sing, pray, contribute money, and feel respectable. Suffering is not on their list of what happens to Christians. Their minds have not comprehended that Christians are to be like Christ.

As Christ suffered, Christians must also suffer. In America, Christians' suffering is usually when they lose their respectability among the 'intellectuals.' Christians do not get abortions, practice immorality, believe in evolution, or cheat on their taxes. They maintain their integrity and remain whole in God's sight. However, in the sight of mainstream intellectuals, Christians do not have a very high I.Q. and would be much better off if they would "Curse God and die" to their steadfast belief in God, and place their life in their own hands, selfishly seek their own betterment, and be friends of those who have put God out of their lives. As Job kept his integrity, Christians also have the resolve to keep their integrity in spite of what satan and his temptations hurl into their path.

God rewarded Job by giving him twice the wealth that he once had. According to ancient folklore Mrs. Job died and Job married Dinah, the daughter of the patriarch Jacob. She was the mother of Job's second family. They begat a clan of people who believed in God and did not become idol worshippers as did most of the world at that time. The new Mrs. Job joyfully joined Job in maintaining integrity toward God and worshipping HIM.

***

Virgin Daughter of Zion, the Daughter of Jerusalem

(When the Bible states something twice, Christians need to take notice and study both passages carefully. That is why this woman is included in this chapter.)

Sennacherib of Assyria conquered much of Israel during the time Isaiah was God's prophet and Hezekiah was king. He and his powerful army were near Jerusalem when Sennacherib sent this message to King Hezekiah and to those living in Jerusalem. Sennacherib did not believe in or serve the God of the Hebrews, he served idols. His was a fearful message telling them that they were going to all be killed and he would destroy the place of worship of the God of Abraham, Isaac and Jacob. He fully trusted his idol gods to make him victorious.

"Do not let the God you depend on deceive you when he says Jerusalem will not be handed over to the King of Assyria. Surely you have heard what the kings of Assyria have done to the countries, destroying them completely. And you will be delivered? Did the gods of the nations that were destroyed by my forefathers deliver them--"

(II Kings18 & Isaiah 37:9-12a)

Hezekiah took the letter from Sennacherib and went to the temple of God and spread the letter before HIM and reverently prayed for deliverance. God answered by saying:

This is the word that the LORD has spoken against him:
The virgin daughter of Zion
despises and mocks you.
The Daughter of Jerusalem
tosses her head as you flee.
Who is it you have insulted and blasphemed?
Against whom have you raised your voice
and lifted your eyes in pride?
Against the Holy One of Israel!
By your messages you have heaped insults on the Lord.
(II Kings 19:21 & Isaiah 37:22-24a)

...

Once more a remnant of the house of Judah will take root below and bear fruit above. For out of Jerusalem will come a remnant
and out of Mount Zion a band of survivors.
The zeal of the LORD Almighty
will accomplish this.
(II Kings 19:21-22 & Isaiah 37:31-21)

The reading in II Kings does not include Isaiah 37:32. The narrative in II Kings records the history. Isaiah records the history as well as telling the significance of the event. It was a sign pointing to the coming of God's son, Jesus.

The Virgin Daughter of Zion, also called the Daughter of Jerusalem, is the church that Jesus bought with HIS own blood. As God was going to prevent Sennacherib from entering Jerusalem at that time, HE will also prevent the Church from being overcome by evil ones who do not worship HIM. Christians can "toss their heads' at any threat that is made to the Church. God will make sure that the evil ones who attack it will flee and then be destroyed. Rejoice Christians! We will not be overcome by evil ones, even if we die standing up for Jesus. It may seem as impossible as Sarah having Isaac at age ninety years old, but God will deliver us. As God made Sarah to laugh, HE will make Christians laugh.

***

Elizabeth, The Mother Of John The Baptist

At that time Mary got ready and hurried to a town in the hill country of Judah, where she entered Zechariah's home and greeted Elizabeth. When Elizabeth heard Mary's greeting, the baby leaped in her womb and Elizabeth was filled with the Holy Spirit. In a loud voice she exclaimed: "Blessed are you among women, and blessed is the child you will bear! But why am I so favored that the mother of my Lord should come to me? As soon as the sound of your greeting reached my ears, the baby in my womb leaped for joy. Blessed is she who has believed that what the Lord has said to her will be accomplished.

(Luke 1:39-45)

The word, Elizabeth, in the Hebrew is "God is my oath" or "God is a covenant maker," She was a descendant of Aaron, the first high priest, whose wife was also named, Elizabeth. Both Elizabeth and her husband

Zechariah were elderly, past the age of having children. They had never had any children, she was considered barren.

Her husband, Zechariah, was a priest who served at the temple in Jerusalem. There were twenty-four divisions of priests and each division served one week every six months. During one of his weeks of service, an angel appeared to Zechariah and told him that he and Elizabeth would have a son and that they were to name him John. As a sign that this would surely happen, Zechariah would not be able to speak a work until the child was born.

When Mary heard that she, a virgin, was to be the woman who would bear the Messiah, she was overjoyed. She went to see Elizabeth.

Almost all of the Jews in Israel knew that Zechariah had seen an angel and was not able to speak a word about it. Some commentaries say that Mary and Elizabeth were cousins. Since Mary had herself seen an angel, it is not surprising that she would make arrangements to visit Elizabeth and Zechariah.

As soon as Mary greeted Elizabeth, her baby leaped within her womb. And Elizabeth was filled with the Holy Spirit. Mary sang a song of praise to God that is now heard every Christmas. Elizabeth was among the first to hear Mary sing the song herself.

The evening meal at Elizabeth's and Zechariah's house on the day that Mary arrived to visit them had to be one of the most interesting in all of history. Zechariah could not speak, but he could hear. Mary was very careful to relate to them everything Gabriel told her. They knew the Scriptures and realized that they were the most blessed three people that had ever been born. How they rejoiced in the LORD!

When John, the Baptist was born, God gave Zechariah the ability to speak again. Later Mary married Joseph and gave birth to Jesus. Elizabeth probably got to see baby Jesus, but the Bible does not record that she did. Elizabeth and Mary were not able to visit back and forth and rear their babies together. When Jesus was a young infant Mary and Joseph had to flee to Egypt to keep King Herod from killing baby Jesus.

When one examines Elizabeth's status in life, it can be seen she was truly devoted to God. As the wife of a prominent priest who served in the temple in Jerusalem, she had money and position. She had the ability to raise John in a fashion that would be considered upper middle class or high class today. Instead John chose to wear rough clothing, eat frugally, and suffer the taunts and scornful laughter of many of the Jews who lived in Israel at that time. He did not waver at his God-appointed task of being the forerunner of the Messiah. He was killed because he preached the truth to the king. It is not known if Elizabeth was still alive when her son was killed, but her legacy lives on, she did an outstanding job as a mother. In heaven she will live in true joy forever with her son.

***

Mary, The Mother Of Jesus

This is how the birth of Jesus Christ came about: His mother Mary was pledged to be married to Joseph, but before they came together, she was found to be with child though the Holy Spirit. Because Joseph her husband was a righteous man and did not want to expose her to public disgrace, he had in his mind to divorce her quietly.

But after he had considered this, an angel of the LORD appeared to him in a dream and said, "Joseph son of David, do not be afraid to take Mary home as your wife, because what is conceived in her is from the Holy Spirit. She will give birth to a son, and you are to give him the name, Jesus, because he will save his people from their sins."

All this took place to fulfill what the Lord said through the prophet: The virgin will be with child and will give birth to a son, and they will call him Emmanuel, which means God with us.

When Joseph woke up, he did what the angel of the Lord had commanded him and he took Mary home as his wife. But he had no union with her until she gave birth to a son. And he gave him the name Jesus.
(Matthew 1:18-25)

Today the world does not scornfully laugh at an unwed mother. This behavior is new to this generation. Generations before now have a record of many young women being killed or imprisoned in their own homes because they were pregnant and not married. Doctors secretly performed abortions and were paid large sums of money. Even if the couple married, attended church every time the doors were open, had children and their grown children came to celebrate anniversaries, some older person in the group would laugh softly and scornfully whisper to another, "You know they had to get married!"

Today, if your daughter told you she was pregnant, but not to worry, the father was the Holy Spirit. She knew the father was the Holy Spirit because an angel from heaven told her so… you would take your daughter for psychiatric counseling immediately. She would be desperately mentally ill.

Joseph was a good man, but he was not going to marry his betrothed, Mary, if she was pregnant by another man. After God told him in a dream, the father was the Holy Spirit, he obeyed God and took Mary home as his wife. Everyone believed Jesus was the son of Mary and Joseph, except Mary, Joseph , Elizabeth and Zechariah. Joseph, Elizabeth, and Zechariah were all much older than Mary. It is assumed that these three were dead at the time Jesus was crucified.

How they laughed at Jesus when HE claimed to be the Son of God! HE was HIS own witness against HIMSELF. Jesus was crucified because HE said that HE was the Son of God. HE never claimed Joseph as HIS father. Mary and a group of faithful women never deserted Jesus. Did Mary tell these wonderful women the truth and how the angel Gabriel came to her, Jesus was truly the Son of God? The Bible does not say.

If Mary had interceded for Jesus and claimed that he really was Joseph's son. Even if she said she had lied to Jesus all of HIS life, would the Roman soldiers have crucified HIM just to please the Jews? Possibly not; they would have considered Jesus to be insane and left the scene for the Jews to handle.

Faithful Mary stood as close to the cross as the soldiers would allow. She heard every taunt shouted at HIM and wept. Her insides cramped with the tension of witnessing her son's tortuous death. Mary and Jesus knew truly HE is the Son of God. Others who were there who believed in HIM, including the thief on the cross believed because they had faith. Mary and Jesus knew the reality. "Jesus truly is the Son of God."

When Jesus was raised from the dead, Mary knew the joy of touching HIM and laughing joyously with HIM, and being honored by HIM because of her fidelity to this truth. Mary could say as Sarah said so many years earlier, "God has caused me to laugh."

Notes

Chapter 3 Small Groups discussion Questions

Break into groups of three to five people.
Each group will discuss one study question.
One spokesperson will report to the class the group's discussion of the question assigned to them.

1. Talk about times in your lives when God did something for you that in your fleshly thinking was going to be impossible, but HE did it for you anyway, in spite of your lack of faith.

2. Job kept his integrity throughout his lifetime. Do you believe Mrs. Job ever had true integrity? What does keeping your integrity mean in your life?

3. Sennacherib really believed he would conquer Jerusalem, but "The Virgin Daughter of Zion" laughed and tossed her head at his threat. How does this show her (the church today) complete faith in God delivering HIS people from being destroyed?

4. Discuss Elizabeth's qualifications as a role model for mothers today.

5. What does your group think Mary thought about, as she loved Joseph, had his babies, went about doing her household chores, knowing all the time, she was the mother of the Son of God?

CHAPTER 4

SIGNIFICANT WOMAN...HAGAR

Significant Sign...God's Angel Visits Her Twice

•

Now Sarai, Abram's wife had borne him no children. But she had an Egyptian maidservant named Hagar; so she said to Abram, "The LORD has kept me from having children. Go sleep with my maidservant; perhaps I can build a family though her."

Abram agreed to what Sarai said. So after Abram had been living in Canaan ten years, Sarai his wife took her Egyptian maidservant Hagar and gave her to her husband to be his wife. He slept with Hagar and she conceived.

(Genesis 16: 1-4a)

Sarah's beauty was breathtaking and exquisite. Her original name was Sarai, meaning *she strives.* She strove for years to have a child. In her mid-seventies she thought she would die childless and devised the plan for Hagar to bear the descendant of Abraham. Hagar would be a surrogate mother; the baby would legally be Sarai's child.

When Abram and Sarai were in Egypt, Pharaoh wanted to marry Sarai because she was so beautiful. He thought that she was Abram's sister. He had Sarai taken into his harem in preparation for the wedding. God appeared to him in a dream and told him who Sarai really was. God also told Pharaoh not to harm Abram in any way and put great respect for Abram in Pharaoh's mind.

When Abram saw that it was discovered he lied about Sarai, he made preparation to move away from Pharaoh. Pharaoh gave many expensive gifts to Abram and Sarai to placate God. Ancient folklore says Hagar, Pharaoh's daughter, was one of the gifts.

Some ancient folklore says that Sarai and Hagar got along well together. Sarai taught Hagar about the God that she and Abram worshipped. This God, who created everything, told Abram to leave his homeland because the people worshipped a moon god. God was leading them to another land in which they could live and worship only HIM.

Some believe that Sarai, herself, went to Abram's bedside bringing Hagar to him (many artists have painted it this way). Sarai stood on the sidelines and watched the conception take place. Hagar was helpless and could not flee to friends or a government agency seeking shelter. She was Abram's and Sarai's property, a slave. Hagar had to submit to them.

When she (Hagar) knew she was pregnant, she began to despise her mistress (Sarai). Then Sarai said to Abram, "You are responsible for the wrong I am suffering. I put my servant in your arms, and now she knows she is pregnant, she despises me. May the LORD judge between you and me."

"Your servant is in your hands," Abram said. Do with her whatever you think best. Then Sarai mistreated Hagar; so she fled from her.

(Genesis 16: 4b-6)

Most women who believe in God as strongly as Hagar did, are extremely happy to be pregnant. They know that God counts children as HIS blessing to them (*Sons are a heritage from the LORD, children are a reward from HIM.* (Psalm 127:3) Despise is a harsh word. It means to hold in contempt or to scorn. Hagar's pregnancy changed her attitude toward Sarai. Hagar, who had been a slave, was now in a more superior position than her mistress who could not have children. Hagar believed that since she was expecting Abram's heir, she was to be treated like his premier wife. Sarai was to be relegated to an inferior place in the household. It seems that Abram and most of the other slaves went along with Hagar in their treatment of Sarai. Sarai really suffered from being put in a place of degradation.

So Sarai blamed Abram for her suffering.

Then Sarai said to Abram. "You are responsible for the wrong I am suffering. I put my servant in your arms, and now that she knows that she is pregnant, she despises me. May the LORD judge between you and me." (Genesis 16: 5)

Abram tacitly agreed with Sarai that he, too was to blame for Sarai's suffering. He knew the LORD and he knew that the LORD would judge between Sarai and himself. The LORD would judge both equally guilty. The LORD would not put all of the blame on Sarai.

"Your servant is in your hands," Abram said. Do with her whatever you think best. Then Sarai mistreated Hagar and she fled from her. (Genesis 4:6)

Sarai's mistreatment of Hagar is not described in the Bible. It may have been physically harmful, so harmful to Hagar's body that she feared miscarriage. Hagar ran away. Pregnant women who have no money, no friends, and no safe haven do not run away unless they are desperate. Abram could see what was going on, but did nothing to stop it. Poor Hagar, who was not responsible for her condition, could see no other solution except to flee.

The angel of the LORD found Hagar near a spring in the desert. It was the spring that is beside the road to Shur. And he said, "Hagar, servant of Sarai where have you come from and where are you going?"

"I'm running away from my mistress Sarai," she answered.

Then the angel of the LORD told her, Go back to your mistress and submit to her." Then the angel added, "I will so increase your descendants that they will be too numerous to count."
The angel of the LORD also said to her:

"You are now with child
and you will have a son.
You shall name him Ishmael,
For the LORD has heard your misery.
He will be a wild donkey of a man;
His hand will be against everyone
And everyone's hand against him,
He will live in hostility
toward all of his brothers.

She gave this name to the LORD who spoke to her, "You are the God who sees me, " for she said, "I have seen the One who sees me." That is why the well was called Beer Lahai Roi, it is still there between Kadesh and Bered.

(Genesis 16: 11-14)

Hagar was truly desperate or she would never have run away. Now God, the creator of the heavens and earth, in whom Hagar trusted to take care of her, gave her commands that no woman on earth understands exactly. Hagar is told to return to Sarai, implying Sarai will probably mistreat you more rigorously.

To return to the father of her child who gave her no protection from Sarai's spiteful ways was difficult enough to do, and the prophecy about her baby was crushing to her spirit. Hagar did not question the angel; she obeyed HIS command and returned to Abram and Sarai.

Every woman who has ever born a child will tell you that when she first feels the life within her move, there are no words that can express the joy and wonderment of it. When Hagar's baby moved, she probably wept and remembered *"He will be a wild donkey of a man; his hand will be against everyone and everyone's hand will be against him."*

What mental agony she lived through! She loved her unborn baby, but everyone else would hate him. He kicked and moved his little arms inside her body, but she knew that he would be a despicable child when he was born. God never whispered in her ear or gave her a dream in which HE said, "Woman, despise not thy suffering, you are part of my plan and it will be revealed after my Son is born and dies on the cross. You are part of a wonderful plan and honored to be in it."

Hagar did know that God saw everything in her life, and that HE heard her prayers to HIM. The "God who hears" that she trusted was full of compassion. The Bible does not say that Sarai was more gentle with Hagar when she returned. But we believe that Hagar was more kind to Sarai and Abram because of her encounter with the heavenly angel.

So Hagar bore Abram a son, and Abram gave the name Ishmael to the son she had borne. Abram was eighty-six years old when Hagar bore him Ishmael. (Genesis 16: 15-16)

Abram, Sarai, and Hagar all believed that Ishmael, as much as his behavior was undesirable, was the promised son in which all the earth would be blessed. Sarai claimed the child and took him to her quarters. Hagar was relegated to her slave status.

Ishmael's life changed forever when he was thirteen! God appeared to Abraham and told him that Sarai would have a son who would be named Isaac. As signs that this was going to happen, God changed Abram's name to Abraham and Sarai's name to Sarah (*which means princess*) and HE gave Abraham the covenant of circumcision.

What an unforgettable day in the life of all who were connected to Abraham! Every male was circumcised. The men may have understood Abraham's reason, but to thirteen-year-old Ishmael all of these events were traumatic. Circumcision is a very painful procedure. It took several days for Ishmael to heal.

Then Ishmael became slave woman Hagar's son and had slave status himself. Abraham and Sarah were eagerly awaiting the promised child of the promise. This would be the child of promise, through whom all of the nations of the earth would be blessed. Instantly everyone stopped honoring Ishmael as the only heir of the great rich patriarch Abraham. They were waiting for pregnant Sarah to give birth to the real heir.

Ishmael had been born with behavioral problems, and no one really liked him. Because of this rejection, Ishmael probably became more offensive and surely no one could bear to be around him. Hagar's heart was broken again.

When Isaac was born Abraham and Sarah were ecstatic. Their joy knew no bounds. Ishmael, who had been the heir for thirteen years fought back.

The child grew and was weaned, and on the day Isaac was weaned Abraham held a great feast. But Sarah saw the son whom Hagar the Egyptian had borne to Abraham was mocking, and she said to Abraham, "Get rid of that slave woman, for that slave woman's son will never share in the inheritance with my son Isaac.*

(Genesis 21:9)

*mocking (King James Version)
*mocking (New International Version)
*making fun of (Good News Bible)
*making sport of (Hebrew -Greek key Bible)
*laughing in mockery (English Standard Version)
*making fun (New Living Translation)
*mocking (New American Standard; verb-form intensive)
*scoffing (New King James Version)

Ancient folklore says that Ishmael used his bow to make 'mocking' gestures on little Isaac as to how he was going to castrate Isaac. Then

Isaac would never be able to father children and he, Ishmael, would father the many heirs that God promised to Abraham.

Ishmael continued to constantly remember that he was the heir for more than thirteen years. He had seen his father's men castrate animals to keep them from breeding. His character was told to Hagar before his birth. It is believed Ishmael could not control being boorish and unkind. God did not reveal to Hagar her and her son's role in HIS long-term plan for mankind. God wants people to trust HIM.

Sarah witnessed this 'mocking of castration' scene and became incensed. She rushed in to tell Abraham that their son, Isaac, would never be safe with Ishmael anywhere near. Abraham still loved Ishmael and was broken-hearted at Sarah's demand that Ishmael be sent away. As was Abraham's nature, he went to God in prayer over the situation. God knew what Sarah saw was true. God commanded Abraham to send Ishmael and Hagar away and HE would take care of them.

The matter distressed Abraham so greatly because he was concerned about his son. But God said to him, "Do not be so distressed about the boy and your maidservant. Listen to whatever Sarah tells you, because it is through Isaac that your offspring will be reckoned. I will make the son of the maidservant into a nation also, because he is your offspring.

(Genesis 21:11-13)

Abraham obeyed God, although he did not understand God's divine purpose for Hagar.

Early the next morning Abraham took some food and a skin of water and gave them to Hagar. He set them on her shoulders and then sent her off with the boy. She went on her way and wandered in the desert of Beersheba.

When the water was gone, she put the boy under one of the bushes, about a bowshot away, for she thought, "I cannot watch the boy die." As she sat there nearby, she began to sob.

God heard the boy crying, and the angel of God called to Hagar from heaven and said to her, "What is the matter, Hagar. Do not be afraid; God has heard the boy crying as he lies there. Lift the boy up and take him by the hand, for I will make of him a great nation.

(Genesis 21: 15-18)

As Hagar wept in what she believed was to be certain death for her and her son, the angel of God called to her from heaven. The God she worshipped continued to see all of the events in her life and hear her prayers.

The context says that Ishmael was not the usual size boy of about fourteen years old. He was so small that Hagar placed him under a bush and left him while she went away waiting for both of them to die. Ishmael could not assume any responsibility for his own well-being. He was born with behavior problems and normal growth problems. Abraham placed the water and food on Hagar's shoulders in order for her hands to be free to lead Ishmael. Also,

"Lift the boy up and take him by the hand," imply he was not developmentally normal.

Then God opened her eyes and she saw a well of water. So she went and filled the skin with water and gave the boy a drink.

God was with the boy as he grew up. He lived in the desert and became an archer. While he was living in the desert of Paran, his mother got a wife for him from Egypt. (Genesis 21:19-20)

The Bible does not state, but it is believed that Pharaoh was delighted to see his daughter, who had a son by the great man of God, Abraham. Hagar returned to her father in honor. It was easy to find a wife for her son after he reached manhood. He fathered twelve sons, who were princes. Ishmael returned, a man of great power and wealth to attend the funeral and burial of his father, Abraham

After Sarah died Abraham married Keturah and fathered six sons by her. There are some stories in ancient folklore that Keturah is really Hagar. Hagar means flight or wandering and Keturah means incense.

Some stories say he visited Hagar and Ishmael often. Before Abraham died he gave the six sons of Keturah money and provisions and sent them away because Isaac was to inherit the land.

Muslims today trace their heritage back to Hagar. Their history says that she was the ancestor of Mohammed. She is one of their great heroines. Many stories of miracles that she performed are revered by them. The Bible is silent concerning Mohammed or any miracles that Hagar performed.

Tell me, you who want to be under the law, are you not aware of what the law says? For it is written that Abraham had two sons, one by a slave woman and the other by a free woman. His son the slave woman was born the ordinary way; but his son by the free woman was born as a result of promise.

These things may be taken figuratively, for the women represent two covenants. One covenant is from Mount Sinai and bears children who are to be slaves. This is Hagar. Now Hagar stands for Mount Sinai in Arabia and corresponds to the present day Jerusalem, because she is in slavery with her children. But the Jerusalem that is above is free, and she is our mother. For it is written:

"Be glad O barren woman,
who bears no children;
break forth and cry aloud,
you who have no labor pains;
because more are the children of the desolate woman
than of her who has a husband."
(Paul quoted from the Old Testament: Isaiah 54:1)

Now you, brothers are like Isaac, are children of the promise. At that time the son born in the ordinary way persecuted the son born by the power of the Spirit. It is the same now. But what does the Scripture say? Get rid of the slave woman and her son, for the slave woman's son will never share in the inheritance with the free woman's son." Therefore, brothers, we are not children of the slave woman, but of the free woman.

(Galatians 4:28-31)

The apostle Paul's allegory says under the law of Christ, Hagar and her son represent the restrictions of the old law, but Christians are like Isaac, the children of promise, born of the free woman Sarah.

Hagar's suffering can never be diminished. Her suffering was real. But she was a woman of great faith. How much easier for her to bear it if God had spoken from heaven and told her," Hagar, your life of suffering is an allegory. After I send MY Son, Jesus, into the world and HE establishes HIS kingdom, people will study your life and understand its message. Because of your suffering many people will be clearer in understanding the kingdom of God. Hagar, you are greatly honored. "Woman, despise not thy suffering!"

One supreme lesson for us as Christian women to learn from Hagar's life is: God sees our suffering, even if it seems we are alone with no one to help us or understand us. Even if our path is on a desolate desert, with no water to be seen; keep the faith! Pause in prayer and reflect on Hagar's life.

Notes

Chapter 4 Small Groups Discussion Questions

Break into groups of three to five people.
Each group will discuss one study question.
One spokesperson will report to the class the group's discussion of the Question assigned to them.

1. Why is it, being beautiful is not enough for a woman to be fulfilled?

2. Discuss Hagar's radical change of behavior after she knew that she was pregnant with Abram's child. There are no wrong statements.

3. Today, with modern technology, many couples learn that their unborn child will have either deformities or brain damage or behavioral problems. God will not condone that couple getting an abortion. Why?

4. Discuss Hagar's faith in God and HIS reward to her stated in the New Testament.

5. How different would history, even in the USA today, have been different if Ishmael had not had behavioral problems?

CHAPTER 5

SIGNIFICANT WOMAN... JOCHEBED

Significant Sign...Taught Her Son To Know God

Our deepest gratitude to Jeff Loyd. Jeff led a devotional about steadfastness one Wednesday evening at the Cave Springs church of Christ. We heard him and saw the application to Jochebed's relentless effort to teach Moses about God. Many of Jeff's ideas were so good that we approached him about using them in that frame of reference. He agreed.

Jeff was born in Hampton, Virginia, and grew up in middle Tennessee. He is an accountant. He met his wife, Tonia when he was attending Harding University in Searcy, Arkansas. Tonia, also a student at Harding, is a native Arkansan who gave up her career as an elementary teacher to home school their two children Myca and Treyton. They are an inspiration to all who know them.

Now a man of the house of Levi married a Levite woman, and she became pregnant and gave birth to a son. When she saw that he was a fine child, she hid him three months. But when she could hide him no longer, she got a papyrus basket for him and coated it with tar and pitch. Then she placed the child in it and put it among the reeds along the bank of the Nile. His sister stood at a distance to see what would happen to him.

Then Pharaoh's daughter went down to the Nile to bathe, and her attendants were walking along the river bank. She saw the basket among the reeds and sent her slave girl to get it. She opened the basket and saw the baby. He was crying, and she felt sorry for him. "This is one of the Hebrew babies," she said.

Then his sister asked Pharaoh's daughter, "Shall I go and get one of the Hebrew women to nurse the baby for you?"

"Yes, go." She answered. And the girl went and got the baby's mother. Pharaoh's daughter said to her. Take this baby and nurse him for me, and I will pay you. So the woman took the baby and nursed him. When the child grew older, she took him to Pharaoh's daughter and he became her son. She named him, Moses, saying, "I drew him out of the water."

(Exodus 2:1-10)

Jochebed was a slave. No one in Pharaoh's palace cared whether she had enough to eat, slept in a comfortable bed, or even is she had enough water to slack her thirst, and especially if she ever had the luxury of a bath. From her birth until the day she was hired as a wet nurse for Baby Moses, Jochebed had been a slave. But, Jochebed knew that deliverance from Egyptian slavery would come soon.

He also said, " I am the LORD who brought you out of the Ur of the Chaldeans to give you this land to take possession of it."

But Abram said, O Sovereign LORD, how can I know that I will gain possession of it?

(Genesis 15:7-8)

***

As the sun was setting Abram fell into a deep sleep, and a thick dreadful darkness came over him. Then the LORD said to him, "Know for certain that your descendants will be strangers in a country not their own, and they will be enslaved and mistreated four hundred years. But then I will punish the nation they serve as slaves, and afterward they will come out with great possessions. You, however will go to your fathers in peace and be buried at a good old age.

(Genesis 15 12-15)

What I mean is this: The law introduced 430 years later does not set aside the covenant previously established by God in his grace gave it Abraham through a promise.

(Galatians 3:17)

Promise to Abraham at age 75
Isaac born at age 100
25 yrs after the promise.

Isaac fathered Jacob at age 60
Jacob's age when he went to Egypt 130
215 years after the promise

This count states the Israelites were in actual Egyptian bondage for two hundred fifteen years.

Many Biblical scholars write, preach and teach that the Egyptians were in bondage for over 400 years, because Acts 13:20 is interpreted to mean that. But Galatians 3:17 states that from the giving of the promise to the giving of the Law was 430 years. It seems as if God considered Abraham in bondage while he was wandering waiting for the promise before he died.

***

Hebrew oral historians had carefully memorized the story of God and creation. They knew about Adam and Eve, and about Noah and the flood. The land promise to Abraham was known to every Hebrew except little ones too small to understand. They knew their time as slaves was soon going to end. The knowledge of deliverance became common knowledge. This caused the frightened Egyptians to become heartless and ruthless taskmasters. Slavery grew more grueling and merciless because the Egyptians were in dread of the Hebrews.

So they put slave masters over them to oppress them with forced labor, and they built Pithom and Ramses. But the more they were oppressed, the more they multiplied and spread; so the Egyptians came to dread the Israelites and worked them ruthlessly. They made their lives bitter with hard labor in brick and mortar and with all kinds of work in the fields; in all their hard labor the Egyptians used them ruthlessly.

The king of Egypt said to the Hebrew midwives, whose names were Shiphrah and Puah, when you go to help the Hebrew women in childbirth and observe them on the delivery stool, if it is a boy, kill him, if it is a girl, let her live." The midwives, however, feared God and did not do what the king of Egypt had told them to do; they let the boys live. Then the king of Egypt summoned the midwives and asked them, "Why have you done this? Why have you let the boys live?"

The midwives answered Pharaoh, "Hebrew women are not like Egyptian women; they are vigorous and give birth before the midwives arrive."

So God was kind to the midwives and the people increased and became even more numerous. And because the midwives feared God, he gave them families of their own.

Then Pharaoh gave this order to all his people:
"Every boy that is born you are to throw into the Nile,
but let every girl live."

(Exodus 1:11-22)

Jochebed and the midwives shared in the hope of deliverance and going to the land that God promised Abraham. They had faith that God would keep them safe until that time. Sacred to them were the tiny humans that they helped bring into the world. The trio were as brave as any three soldiers of valor in active combat. They protected the lives of their people.

Incredible indeed is the behavior of Pharaoh. How easy to send two soldiers to guard both Shiphrah and Puah and go with them when they went to help deliver a baby. Then take the baby and put it into the Nile to drown. Instead when Pharaoh was told that the midwives arrived after the baby was born, he went into an insane rage and again ordered all baby boys to be put into the Nile to drown.

God completely blinded Pharaoh's mind in ways to punish Shiphrah and Puah for not obeying him. When the other Hebrews were suffering under more and more rigorous bondage, Shiphrah and Puah were able to have their own homes and their own families. Did God blind Pharaoh's attendants as much as HE blinded Pharaoh? Yes, it seems HE did. God rewarded them for their brave stand against murdering innocent babies.

***

It is significant to see that Moses was the son of Pharaoh's daughter for forty years, and he, as the writer of the first five books of the Bible, did not write Pharaoh's daughter's name, although she gave Moses every material advantage known to civilization at that time.

She gave Moses:

*A palace for a home
*Learned modern medicine
*Lessons in writing and oratory
*Education in geometry
*Privilege of bathing in the sacred Nile River
*Fine Arabian horses
*Ornamental gold chariots
*An abundance of royal garments to wear
*Influential rulers for friends
* Exotic foods from distant lands

Pharaoh's daughter made Moses a Prince in Egypt, the most powerful nation on earth.

Moses birth mother was a slave, but the Holy Spirit instructed Moses to record her name and life with honor (Exodus 6:20 and Numbers 26:59):

**She who…lived in a hovel!
**She who…had barely enough food!
**She who…was illiterate!
**She who…wore slave clothing!
**She who…measured precious water!
**She who…had no social status!
**She who…had no money!!!

What could a poor slave woman give her child that would cause him to forsake being a prince of Egypt and be called a Hebrew? She gave him none of the material 'things' that we work hard for to give our children. She gave him the most important thing there is to give any child: She gave him the knowledge of God, which gave him faith. …**Faith, she gave her son knowledge of God which gave him faith!**

***

Historians today are in disagreement as to the real Pharaoh's daughter's name that was mother to Moses. Egypt was in such devastation after the plagues, then the death of the first born, the expensive gifts given to the Israelites, and their army drowned in the Red Sea; that no concrete records have been discovered revealing her name. God knows her name, but HE did not have it recorded in the Bible.

Ancient folklore says that the day Moses was born Jochebed's and Amram's house was filled with light. This was a sign to Jochebed and Amram that their son would be the one who would deliver the Israelites out of Egyptian bondage. The joyful parents and especially Miriam took the sign seriously.

***

Folklore also tells many different versions of how Moses could not speak plainly. The gist of one version is that Pharaoh's daughter adored her baby. One day she brought him in to Pharaoh and put him on Pharaoh's lap. Pharaoh's crown was lying on the table and Moses put the crown upon his own head.

Most of the magicians and soothsayers told Pharaoh that some day the baby would grow up, kill Pharaoh, and put the crown on as ruler of Egypt. Others were not so sure and asked that baby Moses be put to this test. Pharaoh agreed that the baby should be put to a test.

A tray of beautiful jewels was placed on a table in front of Moses and a tray of hot burning coals was put there also. The test was: If Moses picked up a shining jewel, he was to be killed because he would be king and replace the Pharaoh. If he picked up one of the hot coals, he was just an ordinary baby and had no desires on the throne of Pharaoh.

When baby Moses was placed in front of the testing table, he reached out his hand and picked up a burning coal and put it in his mouth. He was treated immediately for his severe burn, but when the burn was healed, his tongue was so scarred, that the scar kept him from being able to speak plainly.

Some scholars claim that Moses stammered or stuttered because he was shy or had some psychological problem. Your author does not agree with them because after God told him that Aaron would speak for him, Moses showed no sign of being timid, or in any way afraid of Pharaoh or anyone else. It is believed that the story about the burning coals is true.

Moses was educated in all of the wisdom of the Egyptians and was powerful in speech and action. (Acts 7:22)

Whatever problem Moses had in speaking, God took care of the problem. He may have spoken through Aaron and this was the chain of communication to the Israelites, or God healed Moses' speech problems and Moses, himself spoke mightily to the Israelites.

***

How did Jochebed teach her son so well that God's truths were so deeply instilled in Moses that he never wanted to be identified with the Egyptians, and identified himself with the enslaved Hebrews?

She began teaching her son while he was still nursing. It is believed that Pharaoh's daughter let her see Moses sometimes and Jochebed taught him every minute she was with him. Because she was illiterate she could not write down what she wanted Moses to remember. Jochebed was steadfast to the task of seeing that Moses was thoroughly knowledgeable about the God of Abraham, Isaac and Jacob.

To do this she had to teach regardless of the threat to her and her family's lives. She did not let fear of Pharaoh's edict deter her in any way. *By faith Moses' parents hid him for three months after he was born, because they saw he was no ordinary child, and they were not afraid of the king's edict* (Hebrews 11:23). Her time with her little boy was so precious that she could not waste a moment in doing or saying anything else than to teach him about the only true God. Jochebed stayed relentlessly on the task.

She had learned about God herself. She was a woman, and lesser women may not have been as knowledgeable as Jochebed because they did not take the time to listen to the oral historians tell the stories of creation, the flood and God's promise to Abraham. She probably asked questions, meditated upon the God who made that tree, or that flower, or that flock of birds flying in the air. She saw the sunset and the sunrise the next morning. She knew God created both the sun and moon and they were not gods to be worshipped as the Egyptians did, but were created by the God of Abraham, Isaac and Jacob. Because of her listening avidly to the historians, her observations of nature, and her own heart in which God had placed eternity (Ecclesiastes 3:11), she was totally qualified to teach her son these eternal truths.

Her desire to teach Moses was all encompassing. Although she knew there was something special about him, she probably did not know that he was to be their deliverer. She knew the time was close to the Hebrews being delivered from slavery and would go to the land God had promised Abraham. No teaching moment was missed. She kept on task and pushed aside trivial knowledge and taught her son only important knowledge. God blessed her efforts because Moses was an apt pupil. Jochebed is a great example today for mothers who spend most of their day in the public work force, but must teach her children about God.

Jochebed died before Moses returned to Egypt as the deliverer. But her legacy lives on today. Her son, the one that she was so diligent in teaching, wrote the first five books of the Bible. *"In the beginning God..."* were the first words that he wrote. To be sure, the Holy Spirit inspired him to write, but his early teaching would cause him naturally to think that the first sentence would begin with God.

***

Today Moses is known and admired by Christians, Jews, and Muslims. Few men in history are as honored as Moses. He is universally known as the great Lawgiver and Deliverer from Egyptian slavery. At the end of time after the judgment, it is believed that every one who has not had the opportunity to meet Moses will stand in line to meet him and talk with him. What a great hero of faith.

Jochebed also taught her son Aaron about God. Aaron was three years older than Moses. Aaron became the first High Priest under the Law of Moses. The office that Aaron began continued until Christ's church was established on the first day of Pentecost after HIS ascension. Jesus Christ then became high priest for all of the peoples of the world beginning that day until the end of time. HE is every Christian's high priest today. It is believed that Aaron did not comprehend the importance of the office that God appointed unto him. Aaron will be of great interest to Christians to meet in heaven.

Jochebed's daughter, Miriam is the subject of the chapter following this one. Her life had so many events in it of interest to women, that it was necessary to write an entire chapter about her.

Notes

Chapter 5 Small Groups Discussion Questions

Break into groups of three to five people.
Each group will discuss one study question.
One spokesperson will report to the class the group's discussion of the Question assigned to them.

1. Why is it wrong to make a slave of any person or people?

2. No woman can hide the fact that she is pregnant, especially after the sixth month. Discuss Jochebed's inner feelings as the time grew near for her to give birth, in the light of Pharaoh's edict that the baby boys must be killed at birth.

3. What is the significance in comparison to Noah's Ark and the tiny Ark that Jochebed made for baby Moses? Remember, she knew the story of Noah's ark.

4. Can your group think of ways to help young mothers who must work outside the home to teach their children about God?

4. Use your imagination. Think about what you would like to say to Jochebed when you get to heaven.

CHAPTER 6

SIGNIFICANT WOMAN... MIRIAM

Significant Sign...Racial Prejudice-Leprosy

Her parents were Jochebed and Amram who were Israelites and slaves in Egypt. Miriam was their first child. As it is when the first child is a girl, she learned to help her mother with household chores. But Miriam also had to help her mother make bricks for the Israelites to build cities in Egypt. She demonstrated early in life that she accepted responsibility as the first child usually does.

She learned about God at an early age. Because she spent so much time with her mother, her mother taught her about how God is the creator of this earth and everything in it. Her mother also taught her about Adam and Eve, Noah, and Abraham. She knew that God had told Abraham that his descendants would be slaves. Because she had been taught to count, she knew that it was nearly time for the Israelites to be delivered from slavery.

When Pharaoh's horses, chariots and horsemen went into the sea, the LORD brought the waters of the sea back over them, but the Israelites walked through the sea on dry ground. Then Miriam the prophetess, Aaron's sister, took a tambourine in her hand, and all of the women followed her, with tambourines and dancing.

Sing to the LORD,
For he is highly exalted,
The horse and its rider
He has hurled into the sea.
(Exodus 15: 19-21)

It is understood that prophets tell about future events, but the word "prophet" carried a broader meaning in the Bible. They told people God's instruction in morality and religion. Miriam was a prophetess, who gave moral and religious instructions to the Israelites. A prophet is also a leader. Miriam is the first woman in the Bible to be called a prophetess. Because Miriam was a prophetess, she was also a leader of God's people.

I brought you up out of Egypt
And redeemed you from the land of slavery.
I sent Moses to lead you,
also Aaron and Miriam.
(Micah 6:4)

Ancient Jewish traditions say that when Moses was born, the home of Jochebed and Amram was filled with light. This was most unusual because they lived in dark slave quarters; there were no fancy windows in the house. Both Jochebed and Amram took the light to be a sign from God that this tiny newborn baby boy would be their deliverer from slavery. They told this to Miriam. This gave her extra courage to be emphatic when talking to Pharaoh's daughter about getting a nurse for the crying baby Moses.

Many times in the Bible the visible presence of the LORD is represented by light. Theologians today call it the Shechinah glory.

The Hebrew term *Kvod Adonai* and the Greek title *Doxa Kurion* are translated "the glory of the LORD." Moses, himself, would experience the reflection of the "glory of God" light.

When Moses came down from Mount Sinai with the two tablets of the Testimony in his hands, he was not aware that his face was radiant because he had spoken with the LORD. When Aaron and all of the Israelites saw Moses, his face was radiant, and they were afraid to come near him. But Moses called to them; so Aaron and all of the leaders came back to him, and he spoke to them. Afterwards all of the Israelites came near to him and he gave him all of the commands the LORD had given him on Mount Sinai.

When Moses finished speaking to them, he put a veil over his face. But whenever he entered the LORD'S presence to speak with him, he removed the veil until he came out. And when he came out and told the Israelites what he had been commanded, they saw that his face was radiant. Then Moses would put the veil back over his face until he went in to speak with the LORD.

Moses spoke with God many, many times during the forty years in the wilderness. Miriam probably saw how her brother's face shone until he put the veil over his face. It is easy to surmise that she remembered how the house was filled with light when he was born.

Although Micah, the prophet, who was inspired by the Holy Spirit to write that Moses, Aaron and Miriam were all leaders of the Israelites who were sent by God, he never wrote that Aaron and Miriam ever had radiant faces as a sign that God had spoken through them. As Moses reflected the glory of God, Christians today are privileged to reflect some of the glory of God with an unveiled face. *And we, who with unveiled faces all reflect the Lord's glory are being transformed into his likeness with ever increasing glory, which comes from the Lord, who is the spirit* (*II* Corinthians 3:18.) This is a great blessing in our lives that is sometimes difficult for us to understand.

Miriam had other names besides Miriam according to the Scriptures. She was called by different names because her life situation had changed. She was called Aharbel (I Chronicles 4:8) because the multitudes of women went after her with tumbrels and dances after they crossed the Red Sea and Azubah (I Chronicles 2:18) which means forsaken because many young men would not marry her because she was sickly. When God cursed her with leprosy (discussed later in this chapter), she was considered dead. After she was restored to health her name was changed to Ephrath or Ephrathah.

There are a few scholars who say that there are two Calebs in this narrative, but this is not your author's belief. Also, some ancient folklore says Caleb married Miriam because of her relationship to Moses. The tribe of Judah was looked down upon because of its Gentile ancestor Tamar. Caleb 'married up' to get a better station in life.

Whatever the reason he married Miriam, the Bible is absolutely clear that his heart was right with God. He was a faithful spy who vocally said in the face of the Israelites wanting to stone him, that they could take the land. As Caleb's wife, she probably heard again and again of the great beauty and fertility of the Promised Land. Their married-life conversations would have made interesting reading to see how Miriam reacted to this husband who had such faith as to fight all of the Israelites except Joshua and Moses. She was about forty-six years old when Moses left Egypt and eighty six-years old when they crossed the Red Sea.

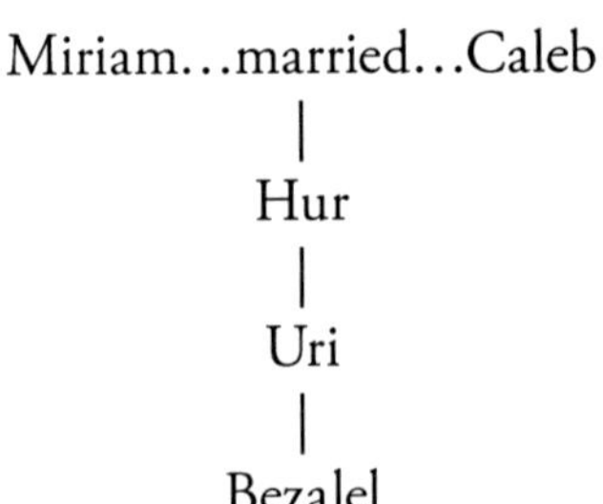

Her son, Hur supported Moses arms during a battle against the Amalekites (Exodus 17:10-12). Hur also served as a judge along with Aaron when Moses went up Mount Sinai to receive the Ten Commandments.

Her grandson, Uri fathered Bezalel, a man whom God filled with HIS spirit that gifted him with skill, ability, and knowledge in all kinds of crafts. When one reads of the great skill it took to engrave the names of the twelve tribes of Jacob on twelve gem -stones that were part of the high priest's garments, it can be seen to what extent God blessed Bezalel as a craftsman. Imagine Miriam's joy in her old age to see the marvelous things that her great-grandson crafted to go inside and outside the tabernacle where God would meet with HIS people.

Miriam's greatness as a prophetess of God and a leader of the women of Israel is stained by one sinful incident.

Miriam and Aaron began to talk against Moses because of his Cushite wife, for he had married a Cushite. "Has the LORD spoken only through Moses?" they asked. "Hasn't he also spoken through us?" and the LORD heard this.

(Now Moses was a very humble man, more humble than anyone else on the face of the earth.) (Numbers 12:1-3)

Nothing warps the personality and one's relationship to God as much as racial prejudice. The covenant-relationship to God is in grave danger of being broken eternally.

Miriam was in deep, sinful, and overwhelming waters. God had spoken through her in some ways, but HE spoke to Moses as the leader of the Israelites. Miriam, although a leader was an associate-leader; never a leader with the stature of Moses. God never spoke to Miriam face-to-face. Also, Aaron was the high priest, but he did not have the authority from God to usurp Moses authority.

Both were exceedingly sinful in their speaking against a person because of skin color. Christians sometimes are no different than Miriam and Aaron. They struggle with feeling superior in many ways. The devil puts feeling superior to others in authority, intelligence, wealth, education, genetic heritage and skin color into their hearts.

Jesus is superior in authority,
…….He has all authority!
Jesus is superior in intelligence,
…….He created the universe!
Jesus is superior in wealth,
…….He has all the wealth of heaven and earth!
Jesus is superior in education,
…….He is the Master Teacher!
Jesus is superior in genetic heritage,
……He is the Son of the living God!
Jesus had a 'swarthy Jewish' skin color on earth,
…….HE is the Savior of all mankind!

God did not delay in letting Miriam and Aaron know HIS disapproval for their behavior.

At once the LORD said to Moses, Aaron, and Miriam, "Come out to the Tent of Meeting, all three of you. So the three of them came out. The LORD came down in a pillar of cloud, he stood at the entrance to the Tent and summoned Aaron and Miriam. When both of them stepped forward, he said, "Listen to my words:

"When a prophet of the LORD is among you,
I reveal myself to him in visions,
I speak to him in dreams.
But this is not true of my servant Moses;
he is faithful in all my house.
With him I speak face to face,
clearly and not in riddles;
he sees the form of the LORD.
Why then were you not afraid
to speak against my servant Moses?"

The anger of the LORD burned against them, and he left them.

When the cloud lifted from above the tent, there stood Miriam--leprous, like snow. Aaron turned toward her and saw that she had leprosy; and he said to Moses, "Please my lord, do not hold against us this sin we have so foolishly committed. Do not let her be like a stillborn infant coming from its mother's womb with its flesh half eaten away."

So Moses cried out to the LORD, O God please heal her!"

The LORD replied to Moses, If her father has spit in her face, would she not have been in disgrace for seven days? Confine her outside the camp for seven days; after that she can be brought back." So Miriam was confined outside the camp for seven days, and the people did not move on till she was brought back.

(Numbers 12:14)

Leprosy causes a person's skin to turn white as snow and then body parts begin to drop from the body. The nose, fingers, parts of the ears and toes. The leprosy God gave Miriam was in an advanced stage. Before modern medicine many babies who had died in the womb lost its body parts because of decay. The Israelites had seen such stillborn babies. They were shocked to see their great leader Miriam become in such a state instantly!

Leprosy truly turns skin as white as snow. It seems as if God thought, "You, who are prejudiced against Moses wife because she is a black-skinned woman, will have skin as white as snow. As the Cushite was not good enough to be your brother's wife, you have an extremely contagious disease and cannot be with your brother either." But the most stringent of God's accusations was *"If her father had spit in her face, would she not have been in disgrace for seven days?"* She was put outside the camp for seven days because her Father (God) had symbolically spit in her face.

No Christian woman ever wants God so angry with her that HE spits in her face. HE considers racial prejudice such a heinous sin that HE spits in the face of the prejudiced person.

Looking again at the incident:

(1) Miriam and Aaron spoke against the authority of Moses because he had married a black woman. This disqualified him from leading God's people. Did she really believe that they who did not like black people were qualified to lead God's people?

(2) God strongly defended Moses place of authority verbally before HE gave Miriam leprosy. Moses was the only prophet that HE spoke with face-to-face.

(3) God gave Miriam an advanced case of leprosy. It is interesting to note that God did not give both Miriam and Aaron leprosy. This causes one to conclude that Miriam was the instigator of the incident and Aaron merely went along with her because God did not punish Aaron with leprosy.

(3) God gave instructions for her to be put outside of the camp for an offense dealing with HIS relationship to Miriam. HE "spits in the face" of anyone who practices racial prejudice, therefore they are to be placed outside of fellowship with HIS people.

Miriam's son, Hur founded Bethlehem, also called Ephrathah, which he named after his mother. The Scriptures do not say he named the town after his mother, but his mother was the most famous woman in Israel at the time that Hur founded this town. This causes scholars to believe this is so.

Now David was the son of an Ephrathite named Jesse, who was from Bethlehem of Judah (I Samuel 17:12). Naomi, the mother-in-law of Ruth was an Ephrathite (Ruth 1:2). King David was born in Bethlehem and so was Jesus. The legacy of Miriam also called Ephrathah lives on. We are blessed when we study her life because of its close connection with Moses and David and Jesus.

Notes

Chapter 6 Small Groups Discussion Question

Break into groups of three to five people.
Each group will discuss one study question.
One spokesperson will report to the class the group's discussion of the Question assigned to them.

1. Discuss some of the best ways to teach a small child about God when you are a mother that must work long hours each day.

2. Miriam's song has four lines and Moses song has sixty-five lines. Religious literature professors have spent several class periods teaching the Song of Moses. Do you think they slight Miriam when they teach only about five minutes on her song?
Does this mean her song is not important? Explain your answers.

3. *And we, who with unveiled faces all reflect the Lord's glory are being transformed into his likeness with ever increasing glory, which comes from the Lord, who is the spirit (II Corinthians 3:18).* Why is this verse impossible to really understand if we own only a New Testament?

4. When we become a child of God our name changes from "Sinner" to " Christian." Discuss the name changes of the great ones written about in the Old Testament. Does this discussion make you understand more why we are called Christians?

5. Why do you think racial prejudice is one of the most difficult of all the prejudice sins to overcome? There are no wrong answers.

CHAPTER 7

SIGNIFICANT WOMAN... HANNAH

Significant Sign...God Knows What HE Is Doing In A Life

He (Elkanah) had two wives; one was called Hannah and the other Peninnah. Peninnah had children, but Hannah had none.
(I Samuel 1:2)

The Bible introduces Hannah in vivid, interest arousing terms because Hannah was one of two wives. The Christian woman reading it today, who lives in a country where monogamy is the law, reads this and breathes a sigh of relief that she is not married to a man who has two wives. However, Hannah never thought of being in any other kind of marriage. If she ever thought about being free from her marriage partner, what could she do to make herself a living? There were no 'career women' in those days. Would any other eligible man be interested in her after she had made the bold move to move out of Elkanah's house? There was no hope of finding an eligible husband because she would be an outcast from society. Social customs are a strong deterrent to anyone in any society, and at that time in history, in that part of the world, it was expected that a man have multiple wives.

But every married woman can identify with Hannah because Hannah had no children. The woman who has born children and known the joy of living in a home that has been blessed with children emphasizes with the pain that was in Hannah's heart constantly. The woman who is married and cannot have children instantly sympathizes with Hannah because she knows all too well the deep sorrow and lack of fulfillment as a married woman. This feeling of being cheated of this blessing in life never goes away.

Year after year this man went up from his town to worship and sacrifice to the LORD Almighty at Shiloh, where Hophni and Phinehas, the two sons of Eli were priests of the LORD. Whenever the day came for Elkanah to sacrifice, he would give portions of meat to his wife Peninnah and to her sons and daughters. But to Hannah he gave a double portion because he loved her and the LORD had closed her womb.

(I Samuel 1:3-5)

Elkanah, Hannah, and Peninnah and her children went to Shiloh to worship. Shiloh was the place that the Israelites went to worship during the time of the Judges. It was located in Ephraim's land allotment. It was there that the twelve tribes cast lots to receive their land allotments. Shiloh remained the center of worship for over three-hundred-sixty years. The sacred tabernacle that housed the Ark of the Covenant was there. A building called "The LORD's temple" was built over the tabernacle to protect it (I Samuel 1:9).

Elkanah loved Hannah. The inference is that he did not love Peninnah, even though she had given him many sons and daughters. If they had marriage counselors in those days, both Hannah and Peninnah would have been good candidates for counseling services. The children were innocent victims. They were probably acutely aware that their father did not love their mother; he loved only Hannah. It can be speculated that they hated Hannah as much as their mother hated her and helped to make Hannah's life miserable.

And because the LORD had closed her womb, her rival kept provoking her in order to irritate her, this went on year after year, whenever Hannah went up to the house of the LORD, her rival provoked her till she wept and would not eat. Elkanah her husband would say to her, "Hannah why are you weeping? Why don't you eat?

Why are you downhearted? Don't I mean more to you than ten sons?"
(I Samuel 1:6-8)

Hannah and Peninnah had been married to Elkanah for several years.

Peninnah felt that she had a right to provoke Hannah because her husband did not love her, but continually and openly showed his love for Hannah. What did she care if Hannah was hurt to the core by her unkind remarks and innuendoes about being barren?

Elkanah felt that Hannah should, "Pull herself together!" After all he loved her and everyone knew he loved her. Wasn't that enough for any woman? What's all the fuss about!

Who cared about the children? Elkanah was their father; did they not matter to him at all?

They all went to worship at Shiloh every year. They did not fail to offer what the Law of Moses required. But only Hannah can be complimented for her behavior. Although she cried and was deeply depressed, she did not lash out at Peninnah, Elkanah, or the children. She went to God in prayer. HE understood her and HE could help her. She is a model for oppressed women today.

It is well documented that Muslim women are treated worse than the family animals, but not so documented that Christian women are living in circumstances in which they are taunted verbally and physically abused by their husbands, in-laws, stepchildren, and non-Christian neighbors. If this is your situation, please follow Hannah's example. Cry out to God in prayer! HE knows HIS purpose for your life. HE will give you comfort. You may live to see in your old age that you blessed some by your example of patience in suffering.

Once when they had finished eating and drinking in Shiloh, Hannah stood up. Now Eli the priest was sitting on a chair by the doorpost of the LORD'S temple. In bitterness of soul Hannah wept much and prayed to the LORD. And she made a vow saying, "O LORD Almighty, if you will only look upon your servant's misery and remember me, and not forget your servant but give her a son, then I will give him to the LORD for all of the days of his life, and no razor will ever be used on his head."

(I Samuel 1:9-11)

There was no greater sacrifice that Hannah could give. She had no son, but if God would give her one, she would give him back to God. What to do about being barren was not told in the Law of Moses. Hannah thought of this sacrifice all by herself. No one had ever given a live child as a sacrifice before. Idolatrous pagans killed their children as sacrifices to their idols, but not live sacrifices in service to their gods. Hannah did not know that she was God-like in her actions. It is believed that she had no idea that God would give HIS only son as a sacrifice in the far-off future.

It is important not to confuse Hannah's vow with the Nazarite vow in the Law of Moses. Hannah knew about Nazarite vows, but her vow was not a complete Nazarite vow. According to the Law of Moses a Nazarite vow meant that:

1.The person could eat nothing of the grape, no wine, no grapes, no raisins or any grape product. Grapes represented joy. A more serious state of mind was required of the person under a Nazarite vow.

(2) The person could not go near a dead body, even his own family. Dead bodies and graves made a person unclean. A Nazarite must maintain a high state of purity.

(3) No razor or hair cutting instrument was allowed to cut the hair. Hannah was familiar with Samson's life. He was a true Nazarite from birth. Single-handedly he killed all of the Philistines, the oppressing

enemy of the Israelites. Hannah only promised one-third of the Nazarite vow. Her reasons for only this one part are not fully understood.

As she kept praying to the LORD, Eli observed her mouth. Hannah was praying her heart, and her lips were moving but her voice was not heard. Eli thought she was drunk and said to her, "How long will you keep on getting drunk? Get rid of your wine."

"Not so, my lord," Hannah replied, "I am a woman who is deeply troubled. I have not been drinking wine or beer; I was pouring out my soul to the LORD. Do not take your servant for a wicked woman; I have been praying out of my great anguish and grief.

(I Samuel 1: 12-16)

When a person is living a Godly life, expect to be misunderstood even by others who are also living a Godly life. Eli, the priest at Shiloh, truly believed that Hannah had been drinking too much and this was why she was acting so strangely. She defended herself and told him what the problem was.

Eli answered, "Go in peace, and may the God of Israel grant you what you have asked of him"

She said, May your servant find favor in your eyes." Then she went her way and ate something, and her face was no longer downcast.

(I Samuel 1:17-18)

Hannah had such great faith that she did not waver when Eli told her to "Go in peace." A person of lesser faith may have asked for proof that her prayer had been answered. "I think you dismiss anyone who troubles you with that statement. I want some tangible proof that I will have a son."

Early the next morning they arose and worshipped before the Lord and then went back home to Ramah. Elkanah lay with Hannah his wife, and the LORD remembered her. So in the course of time Hannah conceived and gave birth to a son. She named him Samuel, saying, "Because I asked the LORD for him."

(I Samuel 1:19-20)

When a woman is expecting a baby, it is normal to wonder if it will be a boy or a girl. Hannah had confidence that she would bear a son. We are not told how her pregnancy affected her relationship with Peninnah and her children. Also, we are not told if Elkanah gave Peninnah more attention because Hannah was pregnant. Did Elkanah want to be just a 'normal' husband in a polygamous marriage? Did he try to love both women equally since Hannah became pregnant?

When the man Elkanah went up with his family to offer the annual sacrifice to the LORD and to fulfill his vow, Hannah did not go. She said to her husband, "After the boy is weaned, I will take him and present him before the LORD and he will live there always."

*"Do what seems best to you," Elkanah told her. "Stay here until you have weaned him, only may the LORD make good *his word. So the woman stayed at home and nursed her son until she weaned him.*

*(The word translated his in the NIV is translated your in the Septuagint and it is believed by your author that your is the proper translation.)

(I Samuel 1:21-23)

Elkanah had children by Peninnah and he knew how strongly mothers love their own children. He also knew that Hannah had promised to give God this child when she had not held her own child in her arms. He was the head of his house and intended that this child be given to God as promised.

After he was weaned, she took the boy with her, young as he was, along with a three-year-old bull, an ephah of flour and a skin of wine, and brought him to the house of the LORD at Shiloh. When they had slaughtered the bull, they brought the boy to Eli, and she said to him, "As surely as you live, I am the woman who stood here beside you praying to the LORD. I prayed for this child and the LORD has granted what I asked of him. So now I give him to the LORD. For his whole life, he will be given over to the LORD." And he worshipped the LORD there.

(I Samuel 1:24-28)

Bible scholars say Samuel was older than modern-day babies are when he was weaned. He could walk and talk. Hannah had carefully taught him that she was going to leave him to serve the LORD all of his life. Hannah was a woman of strong character. She made her promise to God and did not waver or fail to keep it.

***

Then Hannah prayed and said:
My heart rejoices in the LORD;
in the LORD my horn is lifted high.
My mouth boasts over my enemies,
for I delight in your deliverance.

There is no one holy like the LORD;
There is no one beside you;
there is no Rock like our God.

Do not keep talking so proudly
or let your mouth speak such arrogance,
for the LORD is a God who knows,
and by him deeds are weighed.

"The bows of the warriors are broken,
but those who stumbled are armed with strength.
Those who are full hire themselves out for food,
But those who were hungry hunger no more.
She who was barren has borne seven children,
but she who had many sons pines away.

The LORD brings death and makes alive;
he brings down to the grave and raises up.

The LORD sends poverty and wealth;
he humbles and he exalts.
He raises the poor from the dust
and lifts the needy from the ash heap;
he seats them with princes
and has them inherit a throne of honor.

"For the foundations of the earth are the LORD'S;
upon them he has set the world.
He will guard the feet of his saints,
But the wicked will be silenced in darkness.

" It is not by strength that one prevails;
those who oppose the LORD will be shattered.
He will thunder against them from heaven;
The LORD will judge the ends of the earth.

"He will give strength to its king,
and exalt the horn of his anointed.

Then Elkanah went home to Ramah, but the boy ministered before the LORD under Eli the priest.

(I Samuel 2:1-10)

The knowledge of future events that Hannah revealed in her prayer cause wonder and humility in the reader:

*How did she know that she would bear more children?

* How did she know that her son would be instrumental in bringing Israel back into covenant relationship with God?

*How did she know that Israel would have a king, all of Israel's previous existence God had been their king?

* How did she know that Jesus would come to earth and be King of Kings and Lord of Lords?

* Did Hannah really understand what she was saying?

There is only one answer to these questions. God is always in control of our lives. HE uses those who are pure in heart in ways that we cannot understand. Hannah sacrificed the dearest on earth to God and HE used her mouth to tell of future events that Israel's prominent leaders knew nothing about.

Each year his mother made him a little robe and took it to him when she went up with her husband to offer the annual sacrifice. Eli would bless Elkanah and his wife saying, "May the LORD give you children by this woman to take the place of the one she prayed for and gave to the LORD." Then they would go home.

(I Samuel 2:19-20)

Hannah did not forget or neglect her little boy Samuel. His new robe was carefully hand woven with every beautiful embellishment Hannah was capable of weaving into the fabric. The Bible does not reveal this, but every mother believes she did. When she saw him the next year, the robe was probably too small for Samuel and worn thin and tattered.

And the LORD was gracious to Hannah; she conceived and gave birth to three sons and two daughters. Meanwhile, the boy Samuel grew up in the presence of the LORD.

(I Samuel 2:21).

To the ancient Jews, the number five signified grace. Hannah bore five children. Symbolically, God gave her grace in the number of children she bore after she gave Samuel to God.

Grace means favor from God. God's favor takes many forms, mercy, compassion, or whatever HE chooses to do to bless someone. Hannah's prayer is one of the oldest prayers in the Bible. She did not word her prayer to impress readers in the twenty-first century, but today's Bible readers read it and marvel at her faith and God's blessing by putting future events in her mouth.

Notes

Chapter 7 Small Groups Discussion Questions

Break into groups of three to five people.
Each group will discuss one study question.
One spokesperson will report to the class the group's discussion of the question assigned to them.

1. If you were the wife of a man who had more than one wife, how would your relationship to your husband be different than your relationship to him now? Think about kitchen arrangements, shopping trips, etc.

2. The Law of Moses was covenant law that Hannah lived under. Animal, grain, and liquid sacrifices were offered to God. Today Christians live under the Law of Christ. What are our sacrifices today?

3. Have you ever been misunderstood by some thinking you were committing a sin, when you were innocent. How did you handle it?

4. Hannah lived before any weaving machines were invented, before washing machine or dryers, before refrigerators and kitchen stoves. This means less clothing, less delicacies to eat and much more work. Pretend you live in her time in history. What would be your attitude toward work?

5. This group will write a 10-item (Hannah's prayer had ten verses) prayer that a modern-day Christian woman can and does pray today. Compare it with Hannah's prayer. Does this change your thinking about prayer?

CHAPTER 8

SIGNIFICANT WOMAN... HULDAH

Sign Significance...God's People Can Distinguish The Real Word Of God From Fake Messages

Hilkiah the priest, Ahikam, Achor, Shaphan and Asaiah went to speak to the prophetess Huldah, who was the wife of Shallum son of Tikvah the son of Harhas, keeper of the wardrobe. She lived in Jerusalem, in the Second District.

She said to them. "This is what the LORD, the God of Israel says: "Tell the man who sent you to me, 'This is what the LORD says: I am going to bring disaster on this place and its people according to everything written in the book of the king of Judah has read. Because they have forsaken me and burned incense to other gods and provoked me to anger by all the idols their hands have made, my anger will burn against this place and will not be quenched.

Tell the king of Judah who sent you to inquire of the LORD, "This is what the LORD, the God of Israel says concerning the words you have heard: Because your heart was responsive and you humbled yourself before the LORD, when you heard what I have spoken against this place and its people that they should become accursed and laid waste, and because you tore your robes and wept in my presence, I have heard you, declares the LORD. Therefore I will gather you to your fathers and you will be buried in peace. Your eyes will not see all of the disaster I am going to bring on this place."

So they took her answer back to the king.

(II Kings 22:14-20)

King Josiah ruled over the kingdom of Judah long after Solomon ruled. But he and all of his subjects knew well about King Solomon's glory, pomp and riches. Solomon's story was kept alive because people talked about him at the supper table by lamplight, when the women did their washing at the community well, and when the elders sat at the city gate.

Huldah enters Biblical narrative during King Josiah's reign. She was the wife of the king's wardrobe keeper, Shallum. Her husband knew about King Solomon and did his best to dress King Josiah, the monarch of the kingdom of Judah as richly and handsomely as possible.

Hollywood stars and rock stars were not the first to hire someone to help them to look good. "Be sure that the colors are right and the fashion the latest that will set trends for others to follow." The king's wardrobe must have all kinds of fabrics. Expensive all-expense paid trips to go to the Silk Road market to buy silk from China were paid out of the royal treasury. High quality linen that endured washing after washing, so it gleamed white and bright when seen briefly from the king's robes was no problem for the wardrobe keeper because he had a generous account from which to dress King Josiah. Shallum's was a very important position; the king must look royal!

The keeper of the royal wardrobe saw the king frequently. He saw the king undressed and measured him for new finery. Gold and precious gemstone studded garments and ornaments were under the wardrobe keeper's watchful care. Shallum was a trustworthy person, who was honest and had integrity enough to tell the king what was unflattering to him. He was not a 'yes man;' he told the king when something did not look good on him. King Josiah trusted Shallum's judgment. Shallum, the wardrobe keeper, was married to Huldah, who was a prophetess and a confidant of the king.

Josiah was only eight years old when he began his reign as king of Judah. His genealogy was:

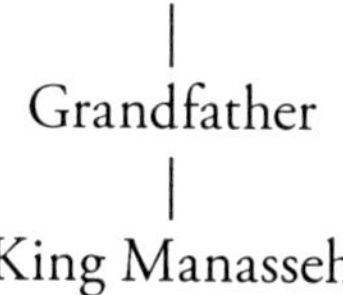

(He was evil, and led Judah into idolatrous worship and killed many innocent people, but was captured and taken to Babylon. Ancient folklore says there he was tortured by being made to sit on an 'iron horse' which had red-hot coals put inside it. While on the horse, he began to be penitent and call upon the LORD. The Bible says that the LORD had him restored back to Judah. Then penitent Manasseh became a really good king.|

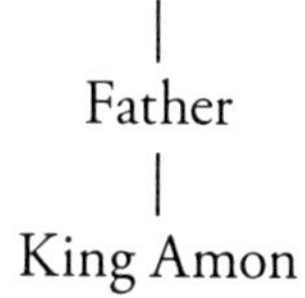

(Who was influenced at an early age by his father Manasseh before he repented and became a changed man. Amon was evil and ruled only two years, and then he died.)

|

Josiah

(Josiah means Jehovah heals. It is believed that Josiah's grandfather named him this because he was healed of the terrible wounds that he received in Babylon.)

The Scriptures do not say how long Shallum was king Josiah's wardrobe dresser. If he was appointed this position when Josiah was first anointed king, he was introduced to a sweet little eight-year-old boy. The boy wanted to be a good king because Hilkiah, the high priest told him how good Grandfather King Manasseh became before he died.

Your author's mother was women's dorm matron in a Christian college before she died. The administration there felt it was necessary for an older matronly-type woman be in charge of the girl's dorm because the young freshmen and sophomores would come to the lobby to meet their dates and bring them in before the dorm closed for the night. Somehow they always wanted to talk to the dorm matron. They missed their mothers and felt better after they talked with a kind, older Christian woman. Mother gave good advice; comforted them when they broke up with their boyfriends and gave them help in their Bible studies. She was very knowledgeable in the Bible.

Since King Josiah was such a young boy when he became king, it is believed that Shallum brought his wife Huldah with him sometimes when he measured new clothing for the king. Josiah really needed a person who knew about God and lived close to God to counsel with him. Huldah could tell him what God told her in a dream and it came true. She was a very special person to know.

Josiah's birth was prophesied about one-hundred fifty years before his coronation. A prophet of God from Judah came to Jeroboam, king of Israel and told of Josiah's reign.

By the word of the LORD a man of God came from Judah to Bethel as Jeroboam was standing by the altar by the word of the LORD: "O altar, altar! This is what the LORD says: 'A son named Josiah will be born to the house of David. On you he will sacrifice the priests of the high places who now make offerings and human bones will be burned on you.'

"That same day the man of God gave a sign: "This is the sign the LORD has declared: The altar will split apart and the ashes on it will be poured out.

(I Kings 13:1-3)

At some point in his early reign someone surely told Josiah of this prophesy. Because if he knew that a prophet of God had prophesied his very own name and birth and many of the things that he would do as king; he would surely seek to find a prophet of God. He would consult with this person to help him rule as God wanted. The only prophet that is spoken of in Josiah's life is Prophetess Huldah.

Josiah was eight years old when he became king, and he reigned in Jerusalem thirty-one years His mother's name was Jedidah, daughter of Adaiah; she was from Bozkath. He did what was right in the eyes of the LORD and walked in all of the ways of his father David, not turning aside to the right or the left.

(II Kings 22: 1-2)

Who was responsible for Josiah being such a devout young child, a devout young man, and a devout young king? Some princes, even today, do not get to spend much time with their own mothers (i.e. England's young princes did not get to spend much time with their mother Princess Diana because they had nannies and tutors on the job from their births.).

Some scholars credit old King Manasseh for teaching and impressing upon the young child's mind and heart to let God be the only authority and guide in life. Manasseh had been so wicked he even sacrificed his own son on the altar of an idol. But he became a changed man and devoutly followed God and tore down the idols he had formerly allowed to be in Judah. If he was Josiah's teacher, he is a good model for grandparents today to emulate. Grandparents have the time and the love to teach these wonderful little ones, while their own parents are so busy making a living.

In the eighth year of his (Josiah's) *reign, while he was still young, he began to seek the God of his father David. In his twelfth year he began to purge Judah and Jerusalem of high places, Asherah poles, carved idols and cast images.*

Under his direction the altars of the Baals were torn down; he cut to pieces the incense altars that were above them, and smashed the Asherah poles, the idols and the images. These he broke into pieces and scattered over the graves of those who had sacrificed to them. He burned the bones of the priests on their altars, and so he purged Judah and Jerusalem.

(II Chronicles 34: 3-5)

Josiah publicly and fervently showed his faith and determination to be a person who worshipped the only true God. The teaching done by those in his early years began to bear fruit and the harvest was bountiful to behold. No more idol worship in Judah!!! Good king Josiah led the Israelites back to worshipping only God.

In the eighteenth year of his reign, King Josiah sent the secretary, Shaphan son of Azaliah, the son of Meshullam, to the temple of the LORD. He said, "Go up to Hilkiah the high priest and have him get ready the money that has been brought into the temple of the LORD, which the doorkeepers have collected from the people. Have them entrust it to the men appointed to supervise the work on the temple. And have these men pay the workers who repair the temple of the LORD--the carpenters, the builders, and the masons. Also have them purchase timber and dressed stone to repair the temple. But they need not account for the money entrusted to them, because they are acting faithfully.

(II Kings 22: 3-7)

King Josiah, now twenty-six years old, took the lead in doing what was necessary to restore the temple the way Solomon built it. It was in a state of pitiful neglect because the people forsook it and worshipped idols.

The reading seems strange that Josiah trusted the men who worked on repairing the temple with the money and had no accountability system. A nation's leaders are fool-hardy not to have a way to know how the money is spent. Otherwise they risk money squandered by workers knowing that no one holds them responsible.

It can be concluded that Josiah consulted with Huldah about this situation. Being a prophetess of God, she could have inquired of God and tell Josiah with absolute assurance the men were faithful. Josiah could speak publicly with confidence; "There is no need to set up an accountability system for the money." Men who are truly faithful to God will not misuse another's money.

While they were bringing out the money that had been taken into the temple of the LORD, Hilkiah the priest found the Book of the Law of the LORD that had been given through Moses. Hilkiah said to Shaphan the secretary," I have found the Book of the Law in the temple of the LORD." He gave it to Shaphan.

Then Shaphan took the book to the king and reported to him: "Your officials are doing everything that has been committed to them. They have paid out the money that was in the temple of the LORD and have entrusted it to the supervisors and workers. Then Shaphan, the secretary informed the king, "Hilkiah the priest has given me a book." Shaphan read from it in the presence of the king.

When the king heard the words of the Law, he tore his robes. He gave these orders to Hilkiah, Ahikam son of Shaphan, Abdon son of Micah, Shaphan the secretary and Asaiah the king's attendant: Go and inquire of the LORD for me and remnant of Israel and Judah about what is written in this book that has been found. Great is the LORD's anger that is poured out on us because our fathers have not kept the word of the LORD; they have not acted in accordance with all that is written in this book.

(II Chronicles 34:14-21)

Huldah examined the book and confirmed that is was truly the Word of God. Some scholars say it was the original law that Moses had written. It was placed on an inside wall of the temple long ago and forgotten. The copies scribes had copied from the original had long since been either destroyed because of the choice to worship idols or not careful in handling it and ordinary wear and tear caused them to be unreadable. Today in homes where the Bible has a place, but is not read often the pages become loose and are destroyed. Soon there is no Bible to read. Bibles last longer when they are used often.

Josiah was penitent, wept and made a public commitment to do what he could to remedy the lost condition of his subjects. He had many copies made of the book. Then he centralized worship in Jerusalem as commanded by God when the temple there was built. He destroyed sanctuaries in Bethel and Samaria that were not authorized by God as places of worship (II Kings 23:15-20).

Because of his obedience God blessed him by helping him annex some of the territories of the northern kingdom, including Samaria, Galilee, and other territories.

Josiah was the most righteous king in Judah's history. He is known as "Good King Josiah." Of course, he was his own man after he reached adulthood and behaved the way he did because he was devoted to God and HIS ways, but it can never be underestimated the good teaching he received as a child.

Your author believes Huldah deserves much of the credit because Hilkiah the high priest or any other of the important men in Josiah's cabinet were not able to recognize the true Word of God. They were the spiritual leaders of Judah and their lack of knowledge of God is incredible. Only eternity can reveal the complete truth of the story of Josiah's life.

Today Christians in America have multiple copies of the Bible in their homes. It is the only guide in following God's commands. Christians must study and examine every thing they hear in religion and see if it is in the Word of God. It takes much study to keep from being deceived by a statement about God's will that is not true.

Huldah is our example because she did not have high position and many servants, but God used her to identify the true word of God. If we study and dedicate ourselves and serve humbly, God will use us too. God will bless all who fervently study HIS word and use it as a guide for their lives.

Notes

Chapter 8 Small Groups discussion Questions

Break into groups of three to five people.
Each group will discuss one study question.
One spokesperson will report to the class the group's discussion of the question assigned to them.

1. Pretend that you live in ancient Jerusalem in a nice house and your husband is the king's wardrobe keeper. This was long before weaving looms were invented. Each piece of cloths was carefully woven thread-by-thread. What would your house look like? Many times when you answered the door, someone had a piece of valuable cloth they owned and wanted your husband make something as a gift for the king. How would this life style differ from your lifestyle today?

2. Discuss the reign of Solomon, his riches, his building the temple, his wisdom and his wives.

3. What blessings did God give to Josiah and his subjects when they destroyed all idolatry? Do we have idols today?

4. The most important attribute anyone has is the ability to make decisions, second attribute is the effect of our influence. How much do you think Huldah influenced Josiah? There are no wrong answers.

5. Why is it so vitally important that a person be able to discern what really is the word of God and not a fake religious message? What are some fake religious messages we hear today?

CHAPTER 9

SIGNIFICANT WOMAN...MARY

Significant Sign...Jesus Is TrulyThe Son of God

In the sixth month God sent the angel Gabriel to Nazareth, a town in Galilee, to a virgin pledged to be married to a man named Joseph, a descendant of David. The virgin's name was Mary. The angel went to her and said, Greetings, you are highly favored! The Lord is with you."

Mary was greatly troubled at his words and wondered what kind of greeting this might be. But the angel said to her, "Do not be afraid, Mary you have found favor with God. You will be with child and give birth to a son and you are to give him the name Jesus. He will be great and be called the Son of the Most High. The Lord God will give him the throne of his father David, and he will reign over the house of Jacob forever; his kingdom will never end."

"How will this be," Mary asked the angel, "since I am a virgin?"

The angel answered, "The Holy Spirit will come upon you, and the power of the Son of God. Even Elizabeth your relative is going to have a child in her old age, and she who was said to be barren is in her sixth month. For nothing is impossible with God."

"I am the Lord's servant." Mary answered. "May it be to me as you have said." Then the angel left her.

(Luke 1:26-38)

There are some today who say that Mary's first child; Jesus was actually fathered by Joseph. The story of the virgin birth is a myth and any person can choose to believe it or not. In some churches you can be in strong fellowship with them and truly believe that Mary bore Joseph's child, not the Son of God. They overlook the statement that Mary made to the angel. *"How can this be, since I am a virgin?"* Gabriel was an angel sent from God. Gabriel would have corrected Mary in countering her statement that she was a virgin, by stating in some way, No, Mary you are not a virgin, but you will bear a son and he will be called the Son of God anyway; hinting…"This is our secret, Mary. Be careful not to tell anyone the truth!" An angel sent from God would know that Mary was a virgin when Jesus was conceived.

Mary is a form of the name Miriam, sister of Moses. Many Jewish baby girls were named Mary. It was a name as common as Debbie or Briana is today. Tradition says that her father's name was Joachim from Nazareth and her mother's name was Anna from Bethlehem. Joachim was several years older than Anna as were most Jewish husbands. A married man must have a vocation and a home because he took over the finances of the household on the day he was married. A well-known tradition says they lived in Jerusalem; other evidence shows that they lived in Sepphoris, near Nazareth when Mary was born.

Tradition says that after Anna and Joachim had been married and childless for several years when they prayed for a child. Their joy and gratitude were such when Mary was born they promised to give her to the LORD. When she was three years old, they took her to the temple in Jerusalem to live and serve the LORD. They felt that they had a Biblical example to do so because Hannah gave her son, Samuel to God. Mary lived in the temple for several years before she was betrothed to Joseph.

After the angel Gabriel made the announcement to Mary that she would be the mother of God's Son and that her aged cousin, Elizabeth also was expecting a child, Mary hastened to go to see Elizabeth.

At that time Mary got ready and hurried to a town in the hill country of Judea, where she entered Zechariah's home and greeted Elizabeth. When Elizabeth heard Mary's greeting, the baby leaped in her womb and Elizabeth was filled with the Holy Spirit. In a loud voice she exclaimed: "Blessed are you among women, and blessed is the child you will bear! But why am I so favored, that the mother of my Lord should come to me? As soon as the sound of your greeting reached my ears, the baby in my womb leaped for joy. Blessed is she who has believed that what the Lord has said to her will be accomplished!"

(Luke 39:45)

Before Mary had the opportunity to tell Elizabeth what the angel had told her, Elizabeth, filled with the Holy Spirit, is honoring Mary as the mother of the Son of God.

Mary's response to Elizabeth was to begin speaking such a magnificent song that many call it "The Magnificat" today. It is similar to Hannah's prayer (I Samuel 2:1-10) and causes one to believe the tradition that Mary had been taken to the temple at three years old.

And Mary said:
"My soul glorifies the Lord
and my spirit rejoices in God my Savior,
for he has been mindful
of the humble state of his servant.
From now on all generations will call me blessed
for the Mighty One has done great things for me--
holy is his name.
His mercy extends to those who fear him,
from generation to generation.
He has performed mighty deeds with his arm;
he has scattered those who are proud in their inmost thoughts.

He has brought down rulers from their thrones
but has lifted up the humble.
He has filled the hungry with good things
but has sent the rich away empty.
He has helped his servant Israel,
remembering to be merciful
to Abraham and his descendants forever,
even as he said to our fathers."

Many people today believe that immaculate conception conceived Mary. Not that Mary's mother was a virgin, but that sexual union did not cause Mary's conception. The reason for this belief is: if Immaculate Conception had conceived her, she did not inherit Adam's sin. This helps substantiate their teaching that Mary was born sinless and never sinned in her lifetime. The Bible teaches that babies are born sinless (Ezekiel 18:20), they do not bear father Abraham's sin or any sin at birth.

In the first line of her beautiful prayer, she said her spirit rejoiced in God her Savior. If she never sinned, why would she pray rejoicing over the fact that she was going to bear a Savior who was hers? She was a wonderful noble woman, and probably did not sin as most of us women do today, but she did sin. The Bible speaks of only one who was perfect and never sinned, Jesus, the Son of God.

This is how the birth of Jesus came about: His mother Mary was pledged to be married to Joseph, but before they came together, she was found to be with child through the Holy Spirit. Because Joseph her husband was a righteous man and did not want to expose her to public disgrace, he had in mind to divorce her quietly.

But after he considered this, an angel of the Lord appeared to him in a dream and said, "Joseph son of David, do not be afraid to take Mary home as your wife, because what is conceived in her is from the Holy Spirit. She will give birth to a son, and you are to give him the name Jesus, because he will save his people from their sins.

All this took place to fulfill what the Lord had said through the prophet: The virgin will be with child and will give birth to a son, and they will call him "Immanuel"--which means" God with us."

When Joseph woke up, he did what the angel of the Lord had commanded him and took Mary home as his wife. But he had no union with her until she gave birth to a son. And he gave him the name Jesus.

(Matthewl:18-25)

If ever a couple had a secret and did not tell anyone, it was Joseph and Mary. Both knew full-well that the baby was not Joseph's. Mary was pregnant with the Son of God!

Shortly after Jesus was born God announced the birth of the Savior.

And there were shepherds living out in the fields nearby, keeping watch over their flocks at night. An angel of the Lord appeared to them, and the glory of the Lord shone around them, and they were terrified. But the angel said to them, "Do not be afraid. I bring you good news of great joy that will be for all people. Today in the town of David a Savior has been born to you; he is Christ, the Lord. This will be a sign to you: You will find a baby wrapped in cloths and lying in a manger."

(Luke 2:8-12)

Mary did not place baby Jesus in the manger to be a sign to the shepherds that He was the infant Son of God, but God used her action as a sign to the shepherds to let them know the Savior was born. HE did not whisper it in the shepherd's ears; HE announced from the heavens.

Suddenly a great company of the heavenly host appeared with the angel praising God and saying: Glory to God in the highest, And on earth peace to men upon whom his favor rests.

(Luke 2:13-14)

God is the proud father of Jesus and no human could have announced the birth of HIS Son as gloriously as HE did. God wanted witnesses to see HIS Son.

God blessed Mary and Joseph with their own children. They had four sons. Their names were:

Joses (Joseph),
James,
Judas (not Iscariot) also called Jude,
Simon,
and unnamed sisters
(Matthew 13: 55-56) (Mark 6:3).

Many believe after Jesus' ascension to heaven, siblings in HIS family became Christians. Bible scholars say that the book of James, in the New Testament was written by James, the brother of Jesus. The New Testament book Jude begins: *Jude, a servant of Jesus Christ and a brother of James.* They concluded that Jude was making claim to James the brother of Jesus because James had become a well-known leader in the Christian movement in Jerusalem.

Your author does not agree with this conclusion:

Near the cross of Jesus stood his mother, his mother's sister, Mary the wife of Clopas and Mary Magdalene. When Jesus saw his mother there, and the disciple whom he loved standing nearby, he said to his mother, "Dear woman, here is your son," and to the disciple he said, "Here is your mother." From that time on, this disciple took her into his home.

(John 19:25-27)

Jesus saw that Mary would never feel comfortable in her own home, because the Bible states that she lived with the apostle John for the remainder of her life.

Now there was a man in Jerusalem called Simeon, who was righteous and devout. He was waiting for the consolation of Israel, and the Holy Spirit was upon him. It had been revealed by the Holy Spirit that he would not die before he had seen the Lord's Christ. Moved by the Spirit, he went into the temple courts. When the parents brought in the child Jesus to do for him what the circumcision law required, Simeon took him in his arms and praised God, saying:

> *"Sovereign Lord, as you have promised,*
> *you may now dismiss your servant in peace.*
> *For mine eyes have seen your salvation,*
> *which you have prepared in the sight of all people,*
> *a light for revelation to the Gentiles*
> *and glory to your people Israel."*

The child's father and mother marveled at what was said about him. Then Simeon blessed them and said to Mary, his mother: "This child is destined to cause the falling and rising of many in Israel, and to be a sign that will be spoken against, so that the thoughts of many hearts will be revealed. And a sword will pierce your own soul too."

(Luke 2:25-35)

Mary and Joseph may have known Simeon before they took Jesus to the temple to be circumcised when he was eight days old. But the Holy Spirit had revealed to Simeon that Jesus is the Son of God. The fact that many will speak against Jesus is a sign that this is true. Even today, whenever and wherever there is a discussion about Jesus, someone or many in on the discussion will speak against HIM unless all the people present are Christians. As Mary was probably totally surprised to hear these words, we today are surprised to hear so much criticism about HIM. But the very fact that there is criticism; is a sign that HE is God's Son!

When Jesus was tried, beaten and crucified, Mary's heart was pierced as with a sword. Even Jesus' own brothers and sisters would not go to Golgotha to be with their brother when he died on the cross. Mary's situation was as pitiful as any woman's who has ever lived. Her son that she knew was also the Son of God was dying the death of a criminal. Her husband, who was also a witness that HE is God's Son, was dead and could not be there to comfort her. Her other children deserted her, but Jesus, full of compassion, while suffering the agony of death, had the apostle John to care for her. She probably remembered over and over Simeon's prophesy, as she knew absolutely Jesus is the Son of God.

There was also a prophetess, Anna, the daughter of Phanuel, of the tribe of Asher. She was very old; she had lived with her husband seven years after her marriage and then was a widow until she was eighty-four. She never left the temple, but worshiped night and day, fasting and praying. Coming up to them at that very moment she gave *thanks to God and spoke about the child to all who were looking forward to the redemption of Israel.*

(Luke 2:36-38)

Anna means favor or grace. Her father's name, Phanuel, meant the appearance of God. She was a prophetess who lived at the temple full time. None of her prophesies are recorded in the Bible except the one that she spoke to Mary and Joseph when they brought baby Jesus to the temple to be circumcised.

If the tradition is true about Mary, Anna may have known Mary since she was three years old. Anna has been called the first Christian missionary because she told all who came to the temple that Mary and Joseph had the child all, who were looking forward to the redemption of Israel had been waiting to see. Her message probably caused quite a stir in the temple courts. They had been listening to old Simon say for years that God had promised him that he would not die until he had seen the Lord's Christ.

The message probably was received with mixed opinions. The people had confidence in Anna because she had lived so long at the temple and had always set an example of Godly living before them, but 'Who were Mary and Joseph? How could any child of theirs become an important person?' They also had confidence in old Simon, but could he be sure that the infant in Mary's arms was really the Lord's Christ? If Mary had told them that she had been a virgin when Jesus was conceived, who would have believed her, even if Joseph joined in with his story about the angel speaking to him also?

One of the mysteries of Mary's life is that the Bible does not record that she ever told publicly that Jesus was the Son of God. Her great friend and confidant was her cousin Elizabeth, who knew that HE was, but other of Mary's relatives and friends are not named in the Bible. If her parents were alive it is believed she told them.

During Jesus' lifetime God announced twice that Jesus was HIS Son; at Jesus' baptism and on the Mount of Transfiguration.

At that time Jesus came from Nazareth to Galilee and was baptized by John in the Jordan. As Jesus was coming up out of the water, he saw heaven being torn open, and the Spirit descending on him like a dove. And a voice from heaven: "You are my Son, whom I love; with you I am pleased. (Mark 1:9-11)

About eight days later Jesus said this, he took Peter, John, and James with him and went up onto a mountain to pray. As he was praying, the appearance of his face changed and his clothes became as bright as a flash of lightning. Two men, Moses and Elijah, appeared in glorious splendor, talking with Jesus. They spoke about his departure, which he was about to bring to fulfillment at Jerusalem. Peter and his companions were very sleepy, but when they became fully awake, they saw his glory and the two men standing with him. As the men were leaving Jesus, Peter said to him, "Master, it is good for us to be here. Let us put up three shelters---one for you, one for Moses and one for Elijah." (He did not know what he was saying.)

While he was speaking, a cloud appeared and enveloped them, and they were afraid as they entered the cloud. A voice came from the cloud saying, "This is my Son whom I have chosen; listen to him."
(Luke 9:28-35)

This is an incredible meeting. Moses, the great lawgiver who led the Israelites out of bondage in Egypt, and Elijah who had brought the Israelites back to God from baal worship, and Jesus, the Son of God meeting to talk about HIS crucifixion and resurrection; God's plan for salvation of all mankind from their sins that kept them out of God's presence was about to happen. God entered the meeting by telling all

Jesus was HIS Son and "Listen to HIM!" Peter knew it was one of the most important conferences that had ever been in the world and he wanted to commemorate it by building three tabernacles.

Look at the list of witnesses that Jesus, son of Mary, is God's Son:

God
Moses
Elijah
Peter
James
John

Today even if a person chooses to believe that Jesus was an imposter, that Mary was not a virgin when the Holy Spirit placed the sperm inside her, they must acknowledge that Jesus lived on earth. The system of dating uses HIS life as a dividing point: B.C. and A.D. There are other dating systems, but globally in banking, merchandising, and other businesses the B.C.- A.D. system is universally used.

The apostle John took Mary into his home until she died. He is the only apostle who did not die an early martyr's death. Every time Mary heard John preach about Jesus being the Son of God, she was there as a witness that could tell the truth about Jesus conception. One can imagine the wonder as they asked her about the angel Gabriel's appearance. Did she suffer morning sickness while she was carrying God's Son? What were her feelings as she went to Bethlehem riding on a donkey when she was nine months pregnant? How did little boy Jesus treat his siblings after they were born? How did she know to ask Jesus to do something about the host not having enough wine at the wedding at Cana? Jesus had never performed a miracle prior to this time.

The opportunity to be the mother of Jesus was the greatest privilege ever given to any woman. Mary loved and worshipped her son, Jesus as her Savior. She suffered as she watched HIM die, and rejoiced greatly when she saw Jesus after HIS resurrection. The Bible does not record this reunion, but it must have been loving and unforgettable.

Today Christians who have Christian loved ones in their graves live with the hope that there is a great reunion because there are so many valid witnesses stating Jesus is truly the Son of God.

Notes

Chapter 9 Small Groups Discussion Questions

Break into groups of three to five people.
Each group will discuss one study question.
One spokesperson will report to the class the group's discussion of the question assigned to them.

1. If your teen-aged daughter or sister came in and told you that she was pregnant, but not to worry, the father is the Holy Spirit, what would your reaction be? Does this help you to understand why God also told Joseph and Elizabeth about Jesus?

2. Hannah dedicated her son Samuel to the work of the LORD and Mary's parents followed her example by putting Mary at the temple of God to work and learn. How can parents today dedicate their children to the work of the LORD?

3. Jesus was the perfect Son of God. He obeyed his parents; HE never went through a rebellious teen-ager period. Mary's other children were not perfect. Do you think that Mary had to work on not being partial to Jesus?

4. What do you think were Anna's and Simeon's behavior when they saw Mary and Joseph bringing their four other sons to the temple for any occasion?

5. Discuss the importance of the event on the Mount of Transfiguration to a Christian's life today

Chapter 10

Significant Woman...Mary Magdalene

Significant Sign...Role Model For Christian Women

There is no record of Mary Magdalene's parents, husband or children, yet she is a role model for every Christian woman. She met Jesus as HE was traveling and preaching the coming of the Kingdom of God.

After this, Jesus traveled about from one town and village to another, proclaiming the good news of the kingdom of God. The twelve were with him, and also some other women who had been cured of evil spirits and diseases. Mary (called Magdalene) from whom seven demons had come out; Joanna, the wife of Cuza, the manager of Herod's household; Susanna; and many others. These women were helping to support them out of their own means.

(Luke 8:1-3)

She is introduced as a woman whom Jesus cast out seven devils. Much has been written about the nature of these devils. Was the term seven devils meant to be that she was possessed of all kinds of evil...or did the term mean seven kinds of evil spirits dwelt in her causing mental illness and/or deep depression?

Mary Magdalene did not say "Thank You" to Jesus for cleansing her of the demons, and go on her way. She showed her gratitude by becoming active in the work of helping others.. Christian women today are cleansed from their sins at baptism (Acts 2:38). Helping others and telling others about Jesus show our gratitude to HIM.

Mary used what she had at hand, money and social position. She was a friend with women of high social position, even in Herod's household. If she was married, her husband was not stingy with the money; if she was an heiress in her own right, she freely gave the money to help Jesus and the twelve apostles:

Peter, fishermen
Andrew, fisherman
James, fisherman
John, fisherman
Phillip, occupation unknown
Bartholomew, occupation unknown
Matthew, tax collector
Thomas, occupation unknown
James, the son of Alphaeus, occupation unknown
Simon, the Zealot, believed to have been part of a
band of people that fought Roman rule
Judas, the son of James, occupation unknown
Judas Iscariot, who betrayed Jesus

The Bible infers that almost all of the apostles were married (*Don't we have the right to take a believing wife along with us, as do the other apostles...*I Corinthians 9:5a) Look at how great the need for help was. Mrs. Peter understood her husband and knew that he thought he was doing the right thing to get out of the fishing business and learn at Jesus' feet, but how were they going to feed themselves and their family? Where was the money to meet the mortgage payment? When the children needed new clothing or new shoes, how could they buy them?

Multiply Mrs. Peter's concerns by twelve and it then can be realized what a burden was lifted from the apostles and their wives when Mary Magdalene and her friends took it up themselves to feed and clothe:

12 apostles
12 apostle" wives
12 apostles' children
12 apostles extended family (such as Peter's mother-in-law)

Most commentaries state that Mary Magdalene and her band of generous women supported Jesus, HIS ministry, and HIS apostles for about two years. There were probably three or four children, or more children per family and more than one extended member to care for. The numbers begin to add up to an enormous amount of money. There were well over one-hundred people under Mary Magdalene's care during the two year period.

Magdalene is not Mary's surname, it is the name of the town she lived in. When one said Mary Magdalene it meant Mary from Magdala (remember many, many women were named Mary). Magdala was located on the western side of the Sea of Galilee.

Mary left her fine home in Magdala to be a disciple of Jesus. When HE walked a long distance on hot and dusty roads, Mary and her group of women walked with HIM. When Jesus was thirsty and it was a long walk to the next well, Mary and the women with her were thirsty, also. Her love for Him was sacrificial. Her leadership was remarkable because there is no record of the women that she led dropping out because of hardship.

What amazing things she witnessed! When Jesus went to many towns and villages, HE healed all who were sick and infirm. No town was ever the same after Jesus visited it. There were no blind, no lame, and no deaf mutes, Jesus had visited their town. If communication were as modern as it is today, the town would receive world-wide television attention. The former blind, the former cripple, and the former deaf-mute would be asked to tell their stories before the cameras. The person who had been a deaf-mute could speak perfectly without any speech therapy; the lame could walk perfectly without any physical therapy; the blind did not need recovery from surgery and dark glasses, they had 20/20 vision. Persons who had suffered various kinds of pain for many years were smiling and shouting to all who would listen to them, Jesus healed me! There was no isolated leper part of town, because there were no lepers in town. Families were united that had not been together in years.

Then they raved about HIS marvelous preaching. Jesus loved the poor and made the people laugh at the strange antics of the rich and powerful. HE said that poor people were equal to rich people. Jesus loved them and they loved Jesus.

Mary set her priorities; she knew something of great importance was happening. She did not know everything about Old Testament prophesies being fulfilled, but she knew that what she was doing was too important for her to stop her good work of taking care of Jesus and HIS disciples' families. Jesus was changing people's lives and if HE or HIS disciples had to go to work many would be deprived of HIS preaching and miracles. She spent her money freely and was happy to do so. The women with her were as motivated as Mary Magdalene.

You may say, "But I am not wealthy, but I can volunteer some time at a homeless shelter. I can donate food to help feed orphans. I can take an elderly person to the doctor. I can make a vow to God to read the Bible every day. I can attend every Bible class offered at my home congregation."

If you have not attended congregational pot-lucks, you will be much more happy in your relationship to God and the other Christians if you participate in every pot-luck. Make your favorite dish and take it. Oh, how much you will enjoy being with the Christian women who work unselfishly in the kitchen preparing and cleaning up. It makes a person happy to serve people.

You will never be whole as a Christian if no effort is made to tell others about Jesus. Sending Bible correspondence to a non-Christian will give you opportunities to teach others the Gospel. If you have children at home, an exchange student from another country will do wonders for you and your family. The student will go to church with you and see you reading the Bible and ask questions. You and your family will love being soul-winners. Telling others about Jesus makes a person whole.

***

Near the cross of Jesus stood his mother, his mother's sister, Mary the wife of Clopas, and Mary Magdalene. (John 19:25)

Mary Magdalene never left and went home like most of the disciples when Jesus was condemned to death. She went to Jesus' mother and stayed with her. Jesus' mother, Mary Magdalene, and the little group of women stayed as close to Jesus as they could. None of Jesus' siblings are recorded in Scripture as being any where near the cross. All the comfort that Jesus' mother had was the loyal group of women and John, the apostle.

With a loud cry, Jesus breathed his last.

The curtain of the temple was torn in two from top to bottom. And the centurion who stood there in front of Jesus, heard his cry and saw how he died, he said, "Surely this man was the Son of God!"

Some women watching from a distance. Among them were Mary Magdalene, Mary the mother of James, the younger, and of Joses and Salome. In Galilee these women had followed him and cared for his needs. Many other women who had come up with him to Jerusalem were also there. (Mark 15: 37-41)

Of Jesus' disciples and friends, only a few women stayed with HIM until HE died. They had no sinful pride to keep them from acknowledging that they were Jesus' friends. HIS mother suffered intensely because she truly knew that HE is the Son of God. Jesus died because HE acknowledged to the authorities He was the Son of God. Mary Magdalene cared not what her rich and powerful friends said about her or to her because she stayed as close to the cross as she could.

***

The Gospels all record that Jesus was resurrected from the dead, but the Gospel written by John gives a more detailed account concerning Mary Magdalene.

Early on the first day of the week, while it was still dark, Mary Magdalene went to the tomb and saw that the stone had been removed from the entrance. So she came running to Simon Peter and the other disciple, the one Jesus loved and said, "they have taken the Lord out of the tomb, and we do not know where they put him."

So Peter and the other disciple started for the tomb. Both were running, but the other disciple outran Peter and reached the tomb first. He bent over and looked at the strips of linen lying there but did not go in. Then Simon Peter, who was behind him, arrived and went into the tomb. He saw the strips of linen lying there, as well as the burial cloth that had been around Jesus' head. The cloth was folded up by itself, separate from the linen. Finally the other disciple who had reached the tomb first, also went inside. He saw and believed. (They still did not understand from Scripture that Jesus had to rise from the dead.)

Then the disciples went back to their homes, but Mary stood outside the tomb crying. As she wept she bent over to look into the tomb and saw two angels in white, seated where Jesus' body had been, one at the head and the other at the foot.

They asked her, "Woman why are you crying?"

"They have taken my Lord," she said, "and I don't know where they have put him." At this, she turned around and saw Jesus standing there, but she did not realize that it was Jesus. (John 29: 1-14)

At this point in her life Mary Magdalene had enough faith in her heart to make a statement to strangers that Jesus was her Lord. She had not seen the risen Savior, but she knew what power Jesus had and the miracles HE did. She unhesitatingly told them Jesus was her Lord.

She is an outstanding role model for Christian women. We have not seen the risen Jesus, but we do have the written word of many witnesses that have seen HIM. We know by the word of God, that He lives in us and makes intercession to GOD on our behalf. We have more information than Mary had, and this knowledge causes us to declare our faith to strangers also.

"Woman," he said, "why are you crying? Who is it you are looking for?" (John 20: 15a)

The very first word that Jesus said to a human after HE was resurrected was, "Woman. " Eve, a woman in the Garden of Eden was the first human to sin. So God in love, arranged for the first word that Jesus said to a human after Jesus was risen from the dead to be, "Woman." Speaking not to just any woman, but a woman who had declared to strangers, Jesus was her Lord.

Thinking he was the gardener, she said, "Sir, if you have carried him away, tell me where you have put him, and I will get him."

Jesus said to her," Mary."

She turned to him and cried out in Aramaic, "Rabboni!"(which means Teacher).

Jesus said, "Do not hold on to me, for I have not yet returned to the Father. Go instead to my brothers and tell them, 'I am returning to my Father and your Father, to my God and your God.'"

Mary Magdalene went to the disciples with the news: "I have seen the Lord!" And she told them that he had said these things to her." (John 20:15b-18)

Mary Magdalene received a 'commission' from Jesus, not the Great Commission given to every Christian, but a commission to go and tell the disciples that HE was risen from the dead.

When they came back from the tomb, they told these things to the Eleven and to all the others. It was Mary Magdalene, Joanna, Mary the mother of James, and the others with them who told this to the apostles. But they did not believe the women, because the words seemed to them like nonsense. Peter, however, went up to the tomb. Bending over he saw the strips of linen lying by themselves, and he went away, wondering to himself what had happened.

(Luke 24: 9-11)

It is believed that Mary Magdalene was with those in the upper room with the apostles waiting for the Holy Spirit to come upon the apostles (Acts 1: 14). It is also believed that she was one of the three-thousand who were baptized on the Day of Pentecost when the church was established.

The Scriptures are silent about the remainder of her life, but stories abound about her in secular works. Pope Gregory in the 6th century was the first to tell the story that she was a sinful woman, a prostitute, when Jesus cast the seven demons from her. In 1969 the Vatican repudiated the story that Mary Magdalene was a prostitute when Jesus met her.

In many books the authors have said that ancient folklore says she was married to Jesus. The Bible teaches against this and states that the church is the bride of Christ, not Mary Magdalene. They say she wrote the Gospel of John and she was the disciple that Jesus loved and this proves that they were married. It is hard to believe that this was ever fabricated and told. because there is so much proof that the apostle John wrote that Gospel.

The Bible teaches that Jesus cast out seven demons from Mary Magdalene and she was grateful. She left her former life of luxury and became a 'road warrior,' who traveled with Jesus and HIS disciples, enduring the same hardships as they. It can be deducted that she was righteous in her demeanor, inspirational in her speech, a comforter in sorrow, valiant in troubling times, and wonderfully generous with her money. Because of her example, we have a role model showing us how to live the Christian life. We are blessed!

Notes

Chapter 10 Small Groups Discussion Questions

Break into small groups of three to five people.
Each group will discuss one study question.
One spokesperson will report to the class the group's discussion of the question assigned to them.

1. Mary Magdalene gathered up a group of women to fulfill a need. Clara Barton started the Red Cross. Emma Willard crusaded for females to get an education. All a woman needs to start a group of women to doing a good work is the 'want to.' What does your group think would be a good project for some women to do?

2. Discuss what your group believes the seven devils that inhabited Mary Magdalene were. There are no wrong answers.

3. If your group were asked to take care of more than one-hundred people's needs for two years, would you need to count the cost? Do you think Mary counted the cost or went ahead on faith?

4. Mary Magdalene set her priorities and followed through with those priorities guiding her life. Write a list of your group's priorities that guide your life. How do they compare to Mary's?

5. What does it mean to you as a group or to each of you personally that the first person Jesus spoke to was a woman and the first word that he said was woman? To your author, this event shows the completeness of the Word of God. There are no unimportant events recorded in the Bible. Please think about it and state your thoughts.

CHAPTER 11

SIGNIFICANT WOMAN... PILATE'S WIFE

Significant Sign...Light: Jesus the Light Of The World

Her name was Claudia, a family name. Augustus Caesar was her grandfather. Her mother was Julia, daughter of Augustus. Claudia was an illegitimate daughter of Julia. Most historians say she was born in what is now Britain. Some say her real father was Jewish who lived in what is now Scotland.

Pilate's heritage was also Scottish. Other legends say Germany and Italy, however, in Fortingall, Scotland a site is commorated today as his birthplace. The Roman Empire had extended to Britain by the Roman conquest in 55 B.C.

A consensus of the historical writings shows that Pilate was an exceedingly ambitious, talented, and cruel man who had a charming way with words. It is believed he traveled from Scotland, to France, to Rome where he impressed the Caesar with his ambition and ability to get things done by whatever means.

Her marriage may have been arranged. However, if Pilate wanted to marry into royalty with little or no credentials, he could have courted her in such a romantic fashion that certainly she would willingly have married this brilliant ambitious man from Scotland. She could not qualify for a truly royal marriage because of her illegitimacy.

Her grandfather, Augustus Caesar did not confer kingship in Archelaus, when he appointed him ruler of Judea, Samaria, and Idumea. Jerusalem had become a chaotic city. Archelaus was a despotic ruler, as his father, the infamous Herod, who had all of the baby boys murdered had been. The Jews hated him and revolted against him, so Archelaus had many hundreds of Jews massacred. To Augustus the entire region was in revolt. He removed Archelaus from Judea in 6 A.D.

Augustus' successor, Tiberius Claudius Caesar, appointed Pontius Pilate as a military prefect to rule over Judea in 14 A.D. This seemed to be a perfect selection. Pilate was a strong military leader who had an 'ideal' wife. The canny Tiberius believed that a ruler with a Jewish wife would cause the Jewish revolutionaries to be more peaceful. Claudia, who had been on the outskirts of royalty because of her illegitimacy, would welcome the role of a ruler's wife and she would keep Rome's interests at heart. Pilate was thrilled to get the appointment. To Tiberius Caesar, he had made a win-win decision. He ruled for twenty-three years.

Pilate and Claudia lived in Caesarea. Herod, the great, built this city on the Mediterranean Sea Coast between Joppa and Dora. It took twelve years to build. Caesar's statues were there because the Jews did not allow any images that were worshipped as god in Jerusalem.

Any counselor who has worked with those that do not know their parental heritage can tell you that there is an inner drive in any person to want to know who their mother and/or father is if they have not known them growing up. Claudia was in the land that God had given to her ancestors Abraham, Isaac, and Jacob. She could not help being interested in the Jews there. These were her father's people and her people!

Claudia did not know the adulterous circumstances of her conception, maybe she believed that her father loved Julia, her mother, and was refused permission to marry her.

Most ancient historians record Julia's life in this manner:

...At a young age Julia was engaged to the son of Mark Antony.

..... The engagement was broken. ...She married her first cousin Claudius Marcellus. ...He died leaving her a widow at aged sixteen.

...When she was eighteen years old married Vipsanius Agrippa who was forty-one. ... She bore him many children. ...Caesar Augustus ordered her marriage to Tiberius. ...All this time she had many lovers. ...Because of her many adulteries Caesar Augustus granted Tiberius a divorce and had Julia banished to an island where she died of starvation.

Claudia did not have a virtuous mother as her role model, yet history does not record that she was ever immoral. Historians remember her as a Godly woman.

Claudia learned about Jesus after she had been in Judea for sixteen years. Jesus was thirty years old when HE began HIS public ministry. HE was a person that any government person had to know about. Multitudes of Jews were following HIM everywhere HE went. HIS miracles were astounding and the common folk loved HIS preaching.

Then Jesus told them this parable:" Suppose one of you has a hundred sheep and loses one of them. Does he not leave the ninety-nine in the open country and go after the lost sheep until he finds it? And when he finds it, he joyfully puts it on his shoulders and goes home. Then he calls his friends and neighbors together and says, 'Rejoice with me, I have found my lost sheep.' I tell you that in the same way there will be more rejoicing in heaven over one sinner who repents than over ninety-nine righteous persons who do not need to repent." (Luke 15: 3-7)

Claudia was a lost sheep away from her father's Jewish religion. She probably wanted to learn about what it meant to be a Jew because three times a year the Jews went to Jerusalem to participate in their major feasts. Pilate thought it wise if their ruler was there to see that no one fomented a revolution during one of these feast observances.

The Three Feast Observances:

*First month: Passover
14th day … Passover celebration began
15th day … eat only unleavened bread
18th day … sheaf of firstfruits offered to God

*Third month: Pentecost - fifty days after Passover
…Celebrated the day Moses came down Mountain Sinai bringing the Law of Moses

*Seventh month: Tabernacles
1st day…blowing of the trumpets

10th day …Day of Atonement The Most holy day of the year for Jews
…The high priest entered the Holies of Holies
(the place where the Ark of the Covenant was placed and the
Ten Commandments were kept until they disappeared during
the Babylonian captivity) only the high priest could enter and
he was allowed to go only on this one day of the year.

*15-21st days…Tabernacles
…the Jews put up temporary shelters and stayed in them for seven days remembering that their ancestors had lived this way for the forty years of wandering in the desert before entering Israel.

Claudia also heard about King David, who conquered Jerusalem and made it worship headquarters for the Jews. Because King David had shed so much blood, God would not allow King David to build the temple. God instructed him as to how to build it. After King David's death, his son, King Solomon built a magnificent temple. The

Babylonians destroyed it. The temple that Herod had built was carefully patterned after Solomon's temple.

Because Claudia was a woman, she could visit only the court of the women at Herod's temple. It is believed that as many times as she and Pilate went to Jerusalem, she probably saw the temple up close. As a daughter of a Jewish man, she would have longed to go and see for herself.

She also learned about the prophets who told the Israelites that a promised Messiah was coming. He would be a powerful king of Israel. Her servants were mostly all Jews. She probably heard many debating among themselves, "Was Jesus the Messiah? No one else had ever done the great miracles HE performed among them."

***When Jesus spoke again to the people, he said, "I am the light of the world. Whoever follows me will never walk in darkness, but will have the light of life."* (John 8:12)**

When Claudia heard about Jesus who claimed to be the light of the world and the Son of God, her heart was honest, her motives pure and she wanted to know more about HIM. The Jews worshipped the only true and eternal God and creator, not a Caesar who was a fallible man that died in spite of calling himself a god.

After Jesus had been preaching for a while the ruling Jews became so afraid that HE would become king and put them out of power, they decided to have HIM put to death. They had corrupted the leadership of God's people to the point that the high priest was no longer a descendant of Aaron. It had become a political office that corrupt men could buy if he had enough money and influence.

Pilate had run into trouble on several occasions and Rome was looking carefully at his career, with the distinct possibility of replacing him. Israel had suffered thirty-two riots in ten years of Pilate's leadership.

The day before the Passover began was the night that Judas betrayed him to the Jews. Jesus had supper with HIS disciples. After supper they went to the Garden of Gethsemane. It was after dark. They disciples slept and Jesus prayed.

"Rise, let us go! Here comes my betrayer!"

While he was still speaking, Judas, one of the Twelve arrived. With him was a large crowd armed with swords and clubs, sent from the chief priests and the elders of the people. Now the betrayer had arranged a signal with them: "The one I kiss is the man; arrest him." Going at once to Jesus, Judas said, "Greetings Rabbi!" and kissed him

(Matthew 26:46-49)

Jesus was arrested and taken to the high priest's house. The Sanhedrin was looking for false testimony from any dishonest one who would make an accusation against Jesus that would be bad enough to cause Jesus to be condemned to death. They had many false witnesses, but their testimonies were conflicting.

Again the high priest asked him, "Are you the Christ, the Son of the Blessed One?"

"I am", said Jesus "And you will see the Son of Man sitting at the right hand of the Mighty One coming on the clouds of heaven."

The high priest tore his clothes. "Why do we need any more witnesses?" he asked. "You have heard blasphemy. What do you think?"

They all condemned him as worthy of death. Then some began to spit at him; they blindfolded him, struck him with their fists, and said, "Prophesy!" And the guards took him and beat him.

(Mark 14: 61b-65)

The Jews did not have the authority to put Jesus to death. Only a representative of Rome had that power. They took Jesus to Pilate and Pilate, who had wanted lasting fame and to be remembered by historians had his wish fulfilled, but when the account was written, Pilate's sinful and despicable character was recorded. Pilate was never a hero, never a man of integrity, and never admirable in any way. The Bible records Pilate's character exactly the way it was.

Then the Jews led Jesus from Caiaphas to the palace of the Roman governor. By now it was early morning, and to avoid ceremonial uncleanness the Jews did not enter the palace; they wanted to be able to eat the Passover. So Pilate came out to them and asked, "What charges are you making against this man?"

If he were not a criminal," they replied, "we would not have handed him over to you."

Pilate said, "Take him yourselves and judge him by your own law."
"But we have no right to execute anyone," the Jews objected. This happened so that the words Jesus had spoken indicating the kind of death he was going to die would be fulfilled.

Pilate went back inside the palace, summoned Jesus and asked him, "Are you the king of the Jews?"

"Is that your idea," Jesus asked, "or did others talk to you about me?"
"Am I a Jew? Pilate replied. "It was your people and your chief priests who handed you over to me. What is it you have done?"

Jesus said, "MY kingdom is not of this world. If it were, my servants would fight to prevent my arrest by the Jews. But now my kingdom is from another place.

"You are a king, then!" said Pilate.

Jesus answered, "You are right in saying I am a king. In fact for this reason I was born, and for this I came into the world, to testify to the truth. Everyone on the side of truth listens to me."

"What is truth?" Pilate asked. (John 18: 28-38)

Pilate, who had been gifted with a unique way of expressing words to cause thought provoking discussions, uttered these three words that put him in more literature books, poetry books, and philosophy books than he, in his egotism could have imagined. Many debates, essays, heated discussions and solitary meditations have been generated because Pilate said these three words to Jesus.

Pilate realized that he needed to find a way to free Jesus from the grip of the Jews, a way that the only option was to let Jesus go free. Jesus was no threat to Rome. Jesus said HIS kingdom was not of this world. Rome was not interested in sentencing anyone to death who had a kingdom that was not in this world. Such talk was nonsense, totally irrational.

To ingratiate himself with the Jews, he created the ritual of letting a prisoner go free when all of the Jews were in Jerusalem celebrating the Passover. This year the candidate to be released was Barabbas a notorious insurrectionist. Pilate hoped that they would choose Jesus instead of Barabbas. No doubt, his spies had informed him that huge crowds followed Jesus wherever he went. Jesus had healed people with blindness, leprosy, and other catastrophic illnesses that no one else on earth had ever done.

Herod was in Jerusalem at the time, so Pilate sent Jesus to Herod for judgment. Make the Jews happy, and then they would vouch for him when he needed it. This ploy did not work for Pilate because Jesus would not speak with Herod. Herod sent Jesus back to Pilate.

Pilate called together the chief priests, the rulers and the people and said to them. You have brought me this man who was inciting the people to rebellion. I have examined him in your presence and found no basis for your charges against him. Neither has Herod, for he sent him back to us; as you can see, he has done nothing to deserve death. Therefore I will punish him and then release him.

With one voice they all cried out, "Away with this man! Release Barabbas to us!"

Wanting to release Jesus, Pilate appealed to them again. But they kept shouting, "Crucify him! Crucify him!" (Luke 23:13-20)

Claudia sent a message to Pilate and entered history. Because God's Word will never pass away, Claudia's message to Pilate will still be recorded in the Bible even in eternity.

While Pilate was sitting on the judge's seat, his wife sent him this message: "Do not have anything to do with that innocent man, for I have suffered a great deal today in a dream because of him."

The dream itself is not recorded, but Claudia believed that her message would stop the crucifixion of Jesus. She did not understand how great Pilate's desire to stay in power. He felt that he must give in to the Jews in order to keep his position. To show the Jews that he believed Jesus should be released he washed his hands in innocence, but to please them he gave the order to crucify Jesus.

Pilate faded out of Biblical history. One tradition says that Tiberius beheaded him, another and more commonly believed tradition says that he committed suicide.

Most Biblical scholars say that the 'Claudia' the apostle Paul named in one of his letters to Timothy was Pilate's wife. The reasoning is that the ruling, royal Claudian dynasty prohibited anyone being named Claude, Claudius, Claudia, Claudette, or any form of Claude be given to anyone except a baby born into that dynasty.

Greet Priscilla and Aquilla and the household of Onesiphorus. Erastus stayed in Corinth, and I left Trophimus sick in Miletus. Do your best to get here before winter. Eubulus greets you, and so do Pudens, Claudia and all the brothers. (Timothy 4: 19-21)

Claudia put her faith in Jesus, she listened and heeded when HE told the followers shortly before HE died to follow HIM.

Then Jesus told them, "You are going to have the light just a little while longer. Walk while you have the light, before darkness overtakes you. The man who walks in the dark does not know where he is going. Put your trust in the light while you have it, so that you may become the sons of light." (John 12:35-36a)

After Jesus died, was buried and resurrected, Claudia became a Christian. He husband died an early death, probably by his own hand, and was never the success he longed to be. The difference in their lives is choosing Jesus, the light of the world.

Notes

Chapter 11 Small Groups Discussion Question

Break into groups of three to five people.
Each group will discuss one study question.
One spokesperson will report to the class the group's discussion of the question assigned to them.

1. How do you think Claudia coped with being an illegitimate royal princess whose mother was so promiscuous that she was banished from the kingdom and died of starvation?

2. How does an ambitious man like Pilate win the heart of a vulnerable girl like Claudia?

3. Discuss the differences between life in Judea and life in any other Roman province.

4. The Bible does not tell what was in Claudia's dream. Discuss what your group thinks she dreamed.

5. Claudia knew in her heart that when Jesus said HE was the light of the world, HE was telling the truth. How could she know it was truth?

CHAPTER 12

SIGNIFICANT WOMAN.. THECHOSEN LADY

Significant Sign...The Church Is The Bride Of Christ

The elder, to the chosen lady and her children, whom I love in the truth--and not I only, but also all who know the truth--because of the truth, which lives in us and will be with us forever.

Grace, mercy and peace from God, the Father and from Jesus Christ, the Father's son, will be with us in truth and love.

It has given me great joy to find some of your children walking in the truth, just as the Father commanded us. And now, dear lady, I am not writing you a new command but one we had from the beginning. I ask that we love one another. And this is love that we walk in obedience to his commands. As you have heard from the beginning, his command is that you walk in love.

Many deceivers, who do not acknowledge Jesus Christ as coming in the flesh, have gone out into the world. Any such person is the deceiver and the antichrist. Watch out that you do not lose what you have worked for, but that you may be rewarded fully. Anyone who runs ahead and does not continue in the teaching of Christ does not have God; whoever continues in the teaching has both the Father and the Son. If anyone comes to you and does not bring this teaching, do not take him into your house or welcome him. Anyone who welcomes him shares in his wicked work.

I have much to write to you, but I do not want to use paper and ink. Instead I hope to visit you and talk with you face to face so that our joy may be complete.

The children of your chosen sister send their greetings.

(II John)

The letter called II John does not say that the apostle John is the author. The Christians to whom it was written knew that John wrote it. The term Chosen Lady seems to be code words for the church. Persecution of Christians was strong at that time.

In the letter there is a strong warning that antichrist workers will attempt to get into the Christians homes and try to persuade the Christians that Jesus was not really the Son of God. Christianity's cornerstone is that Jesus is the Son of God. If a Christian comes to believe that Jesus is not the Son of God, he is no longer a Christian. The person who goes from Christian home to Christian home in order to persuade Christians that Jesus is not really God's Son is an antichrist.

The code words "Chosen Lady" were true words that describe the church. The church is the bride of Christ. The apostle Paul declares plainly: *I am jealous for you with a Godly jealousy. I promised you to one husband, to Christ, so that I might present you as a pure virgin to him.* (II Corinthians 11:2)

Marriage is a phenomenon that is peculiar to the world. The angels in heaven are not married or given in marriage.

"At the resurrection people will neither marry nor be given in marriage; they will be like the angels in heaven. (Matthew 22:29b)

God created Adam to be lonesome without a being that was suitable to be his companion. Adam looked at and named all of the animals, but he could not find a created being suitable to meet his needs as a human. Adam was lonesome! Psychological studies show that married men live longer than unmarried men. When Adam saw Eve for the first time he was overwhelmed with joy. After examining Eve he realized that this creature was suitable to be a companion for him.

The man said,
"This is now bone of my bones
and flesh of my flesh;
she shall be called woman,
for she was taken out of man.
(Genesis 2:23)

Because the marriage relationship is so sacred, the Bible says:

For this reason a man will leave his father and mother and be united to his wife and they will become one flesh. (Genesis 2: 24)

***

One of the most striking marriages in the Old Testament that is a sign of the church being the bride of Christ is the marriage of Rebecca and Isaac*.

Abraham was now old and well advanced in years, and the LORD had blessed him in every way. He said to his chief servant in his household, the one in charge of all he had, "Put your hand under my thigh. I want you to swear by the LORD, the God of heaven and the God of earth, that you will not get a wife for my son from the daughters of the Canaanites, among whom I am living, but will go to my country to my own relatives and get a wife for my son, Isaac."

***

Then the servant took ten of his master's camels and left taking with him all kinds of good things from his master. He set out for Aram Naharaim and made his way to the town of Nahor. He had the camels kneel down near the well outside the town; it was evening, the time the women go out to draw water.

Then he prayed, "O LORD, God of my master Abraham, give me success today and show kindness to my master Abraham. See I am standing beside this spring and the daughters of the townspeople are coming out to draw water. May it be that when I say to a girl, "Please let down your jar that I may have a drink, and she says, "Drink, and I'll water your camels too…let her be the one you have chosen for your servant Isaac. By this I will know that you have shown kindness to my master." (Genesis 24: 1-4 --- Genesis 24:10-14)

*Isaac was a quiet contemplative man who was a pre-figure of Christ because of his willingness to sacrifice his own life. Isaac was strong enough to overcome Abraham when his father was willing to offer him as a sacrifice. Isaac could have refused to submit to his father, but he trusted his father's words, "God will provide a lamb."

Abraham's servant took ten camels loaded with rich gifts for the future bride and her family. When he arrived at the well in the home town of Abraham's brother, he went to God in fervent prayer; because he wanted to follow Abraham's instructions faithfully. Many commentaries interpret this chief servant to be a pre-figure of the Holy Spirit and His work in seeking the bride of Christ.

Abraham's chief servant asked God for a sign: *"May it be when I say to the girl, 'Please let down your jar that I may have a drink', and she says, 'Drink and I will water your camels too.' Let her be the one you have chosen for your servant Isaac. By this I will know that you have shown kindness to my master.'"* (Genesis 24:14)

Before he finished praying, Rebekah came with her jar on her shoulder. This was a momentous meeting for all of humanity! The chief servant of exceedingly rich and aged Abraham, whose son was one of the most eligible bachelors in the world, had been given a sign from God that this is the bride for Isaac. However, Rebekah was blissfully unaware that she was under scrutiny of the servant and walked normally to the well. Very soon she will be on her way to marry the world's most eligible bachelor and in time will become the forbear of the Savior of all mankind. But she did not know that then.

Consider Rebekah's character. A courteous well-trained young lady, who willingly complied to give the chief servant a drink of water, and she eagerly watered the ten camels in his caravan. A camel drinks more than twenty gallons of water a day. It was a time consuming task to get them all watered.

Rebekah was unaware of the greatness of the event in which she was the bride. Consider those who were watching her that day:

*The chief servant who was prayerfully observing her.

*His entourage of slaves and guards.

*The neighbors at the well who looked were watching as she made repeated trips to the well.

*All the heavenly hosts were joyfully watching earth where an important part of the redemption for mankind was taking place.

The Bible does not record that anyone jumped in to help Rebekah with such a toilsome task.

Rebekah was unaware of the chief servant's prayer. She was merely doing as she had been taught to do when she was a little girl. It was her nature and training to be kind and helpful, no matter how difficult the task. After she finished watering the camels, the chief servant went home with her and spoke with her family. He gave many rich and very expensive gifts to Rebekah and her family. He also told them of his prayer and how Rebekah had said exactly the right words to him to let him know that she was the one God had chosen.

The Scriptures tell who had a part in choosing a wife for Isaac.

Heavenly Beings   Earthly Prefigures

God, the Father ....Abraham
Jesus, the obedient Son...............Isaac
Holy Spirit...........................The chief servant
..........................Rebekah, herself consented to the marriage and did not want to tarry and stay with her family for a while before leaving to meet Isaac. She prefigures the church, the bride of Christ.

***

The Song of Solomon was written by King Solomon, son of King David and has many implications. Some read it as a manual for husbands and wives because it is so explicit in describing sexual love between husband and wife. The writing is excellent as a guide in that respect.

However, most Bible scholars agree that the primary application is to state that the coming church that Jesus would establish on the Day of Pentecost in A.D. 33 would be the betrothed bride of Christ. The marriage ceremony itself would take place at the end of time.

A summary of the story is: The lookers for beautiful women saw the most beautiful woman in the world and she was married to a lowly shepherd. They capture her and take her to the king's harem.

There the woman wept and was inconsolable because she wanted to be returned to her shepherd husband. The king made three attempts to win the woman's heart; his ego was such that he thought he could win her away from the shepherd.

First attempt: The king used words of flattery telling her of her beauty. This had worked on every other woman he had ever tried it on. The Woman was not impressed. Her heart and thoughts were with her husband. She wept and told Solomon that she longed to be with her husband caring for the sheep on the mountainsides.

Second attempt: The king arranged for a magnificent parade showing his power and wealth. His army dressed in gold crusted uniforms, riding beautiful horses, royal musicians, colorful dancers, and his cabinet officers all bowing before her beauty. Again she was not impressed. His riches and power meant nothing to her compared to her husband's faithful love.

After the festivities and in the dark of night she escaped the palace and went to look for her beloved husband. The officers found her and beat her soundly for her offense.

Third attempt: The women of the court accused her, "You think that you are better than all of us. We, too, had to leave our lovers behind to be in the king's harem. Your beloved is no better than ours.

The captured woman convinced the harem women that her only desire was to stay with her husband. She would never, never enjoy being part of the king's harem.

The harem women tacitly acquiesce that harem life was really not a satisfactory life. They took the woman into their confidence and asked her for advice. They have little sisters at home and as soon as they mature they will be captured and taken to the harem against their will. What can they do to save them from such a fate?

The captured woman, who pre-figures the bride of Christ states:

I am a wall
and my breasts are like towers.
Thus I have become in his eyes
like one bringing contentment.
(Song of Solomon 7:10)

The application is, do not give in to the seductive king with his riches and power. Do not look to others to do your 'standing for right' for you. Her statement, "I am a wall" meant that she would never consent to have sex with the king because she is married to the shepherd and would remain faithful to him.

The woman represents ….. The bride of Christ
The shepherd represents ….. Jesus, the Good Shepherd
King Solomon …..represents evil that would lure the woman away from her loving, faithful husband.

(Scholars believe this event caused a turning point in Solomon's life, so he wrote this true account as his confession of sin. He had married so many idolatrous women who had taken his heart away from God. When he saw the woman's adamant refusal to be taken in by money, power, and position, he saw God using her to help him realize his own sinful state. He wanted to return to God. God accepted Solomon's repentance and had this poem as well as the many proverbs and the book of Ecclesiastes put into the Scriptures.)

***

Marriage is a covenant between two people; the bride and the groom. Each person vows (promises) to do certain things in the marriage. It is also a legal contract (covenant).

Every covenant originates with words, a sacrifice, and a seal. In the marriage covenant the couple pledge their love to each other and their desire to be married to each other for the rest of their lives. Each sacrifices their personal desires and selfish ambitions to the keeping of the marriage covenant. Then as a seal, there is an exchange of rings. The wedding ring is a symbol that this person has a covenant marriage partner and is committed to that relationship.
In The Marriage Of The Bride Of Christ

There are words: The Gospel the death, burial, and resurrection of Jesus. The penitent believer's confession that a person believes truly that Jesus is the Son of God.

There is a sacrifice: Jesus. HIS death is re-enacted in the baptism of the penitent believer.

There is a seal: The Holy Spirit indwelling the Christian.

After this I heard what sounded like the roar of a great multitude in the heavens shouting: "Hallelujah! Salvation and glory and power belong to our God,

for true and just are his judgments.
He has condemned the great prostitute
Who corrupted the earth by her adulteries. He has avenged on her the blood of his servants.
And again they shouted:
"Hallelujah!"
Then a voice came from the throne saying:
"Praise our God,
All you his servants,
You who fear him,
Both small and great!"

Then I heard what sounded like a great multitude, like the roar of rushing waters and like loud peals of thunder, shouting:

"Hallelujah!
For our Lord God Almighty reigns.
Let us rejoice and be glad
And give him glory!
For the wedding of the Lamb has come,
And the bride has made herself ready.
Fine linen, bright and clean,
Was given to her to wear."
(Fine linen stands for the righteous acts of the saints.)
Then the angel said to me, "Write:
"Blessed are those who are invited
to the wedding supper of the Lamb!"
(Revelation 19: 1-9a)

Notes

Chapter 12 Small Groups Discussion Questions

Break into small groups of three to five people.
Each group will discuss one study question.
One spokesperson will report to the class the group's discussion of the question assigned to them.

1. There are many Christians today being persecuted because they are Christians, but not too many in the United States. Discuss persecution of Christians that your group knows about. Can anything be done to help them?

2. The fact that Jesus is the true Son of God is the cornerstone of Christianity and our salvation. Have you ever been in discussion with someone who honestly did not believe this? Please tell the class about it.

3. Rebekah was a hardworking and polite young lady. God wants her same characteristics to be in Christians. Why?

4. How much steadfast love for her husband did the woman in the Song of Solomon have for her husband to make the statement, "I am a wall"...and go on to infer if she ever had sex with anyone but her shepherd husband, it would have to be that she was raped.

5. Read the passage in Revelation concerning the marriage of the Lamb. Consider the exceeding joy in heaven when Christ returns to take HIS own to be seated at the marriage supper of the Lamb. How does this make you feel about being a Christian?

Part II

Unknown Women Whose Good Influence In Today's World Make It A Better Planet

CHAPTER 13

INTRODUCTION TO THE SEAY SISTERS

Marge Murray
Tilda O'Neal
Anna Lewis
Nancy Gammill
Betty Foster
Sheila Mullins

The Twenty-Five Year Secret

This true story was first written about in my book, *Solomon's Legacy For Women* (page 111). It is about Willie and Thelma Seay, who were Christians that were poor in money, but rich in greatness of mind, will, and spirit. They are the parents of thirteen children. Today their children are the beneficiaries of a legacy of unselfishness that is legendary.

Due to the limited income available to a day worker, never above minimum wage, and the number of children in their family (thirteen), Willie and Thelma had never been able to afford their own home. Some of the children saw an ideal retirement home for their parents. They got all of the children together and each child agreed to send a dollar amount each month to help their parents meet the mortgage payment. This was to show their parents how much they loved and appreciated them. Willie and Thelma lived by the philosophy, "*Watch your pennies and the dollars will take care of themselves.*" They had learned in the Great Depression to be careful about spending money.

During the festivities and gift giving celebrating their sixtieth wedding anniversary, Willie and Thelma had a **surprise** for their children. Each of their thirteen children was presented with an envelope. Inside the envelopes the children found a sum of money equal to the amount each had given to their parents for the past **twenty-five** years to help pay the mortgage payment on their retirement home. None of the envelopes contained less than one thousand dollars.

They had managed to pay off the mortgage of their retirement home without their children's help because they **sacrificed every personal comfort**. Their steadfast resolve helps one to understand how extraordinary they were in not being a burden to their children. Their independent spirit and unselfish love for their sons and daughters was "Extraordinary! Yea phenomenal!" To say that their children were overwhelmed is an understatement.

***

Author's Note To Readers:

Willie and Thelma had six daughters and seven sons. Arrangements were made to interview each daughter at a family reunion on Memorial Day, 2008. It was a high privilege to interview their six daughters to record how each individual daughter remembers her parents. To learn how their individual personalities are different and how they are similar. The questionnaire used does not claim to be scientifically accurate, but does reflect their individual personalities and how their parents, especially their mother, influenced their lives.

Soon after it was decided to publish the interviews of the Seay sisters, they were requested not to discuss their individual family remembrances before they were interviewed. Each was interviewed in a one-on-one session with your author.

Interviewing the six daughters of Thelma Norman Seay revealed the tremendous influence of the mother upon her children. The legacy of Willie and Thelma Seay is found in the responses to the surveys each daughter completed in their own words. The strength of character and individualism of these six women demonstrate the success of their parents in instilling Christian values in their children.

They are six individual women.
They have six different personalities.
They cope with six different sets of life problems.
But they remain an especially close-knit family, who are the beneficiaries of a great heritage of love and unselfishness from their parents.

Each is a special friend to me because of her Christian love and patience shown during the interviews. We made a picture commemorating this wonderful occasion and it is on the cover of this book.

Marge L. Murray

Oldest Daughter

Questionnaire

1. Which color do you like best? Do you wear this color often?
Green, or something that has green in it; and shades of yellow.

2. What model vehicle do you like better than all others? What kind do you drive?
Probably a small compact car like I already have that is economical on gas. I drive a Hyundai.

3. What style of house do you prefer? Why?
Ranch style; so I will not have to climb stairs when I get old.

4. Which television show do you watch most often?
Andy Griffith at suppertime.

5. Name your favorite sport and tell why you enjoy it above all others.
Watching football, I like bowling.

6. Name your favorite athlete.
Michael Jordan

7. What is your best loved religious hymn? Why?
***In The Garden*: Because when I was the music leader for Sunday morning worship and I would lead this song and finish with a real high ad-libbed note, all the patients would begin to clap as I began to sing the note.**

8. Name the flower you like best. Why is this your favorite?
American Beauty rose while still in the bud.

9. Where do you do most of your shopping for clothing?
Garage sales I do not like the new styles of women's clothing.

10. If you were wealthy, where would you like to go on vacation?
Hawaii: The pictures show it is warm, not hot like Florida.

11. What do you like best about Arkansas?
Fall season, the friendliness of the people.

12. Tell what Alabama means to you.
Where my father did a lot of growing up. He always talked about it and had many relatives there.

13. What technological invention has influenced you most in your lifetime?
Automobile

14. How many children do you have?
Two: Audra, a daughter and Nathan, a son.

15. How do you discipline your children?
I bluffed them by my tone of voice, "I'm going to get my ruler!" Years later they told me that they hid my ruler.

16. What is (was) you career?
I worked as a secretary and in business subjects for three years before I married. After I married I went to school and worked part-time as a bookkeeper, then full time as a bookkeeper.

17. How do you relieve stress in your life?
Get away from the situation and take a nap, try to get organized.

18. What is the most memorable moment of your life?
When I came home from college after my first year, I was going to visit someone about church. Later my mother told me that she

watched me go down the road and the Lord spoke to her and said, "You're going to need to pray for her."

19. What character traits or attributes of your mother are most prevalent in your personality?
Being able to smile and be sweet to other people.

20. Which of your sisters is most like your mother?
Since I am the oldest daughter and like a second mother to my brothers and sisters, I would say, "I am."

21. How would you like to be remembered after you die?
That I was an influence for the Lord; that I used my education and talents for Him.

22. Tell me about your mother.
I remember her telling me when I was seven years old about the Lord. I asked her who God was and she said, "He's the one who always knows what you do." Then she told me more about God. She would always answer my questions about personal things... about my monthly period, and about sex. Other girl's mothers never talked to their daughters about these things. Because of this I made an effort to help my daughter in the same way.

Thelma was an excellent financial steward. Although there were many meager times, even with modest means, this couple—a product of the Great Depression—clothed and fed six daughters and seven sons very well over several decades. The skill Thelma demonstrated in managing her family finances has to be considered exceptional.

Legacy
Marge became a professional accountant.

CHAPTER 14

TILDA O'NEAL

Second Daughter

Questionnaire

1. Which color do you like best? Do you wear this color often?
Purple and royal blue, yes I wear them lots of times.

2. What model vehicle do you like better than all others? What kind do you drive?
I do not have a preference, but one that gets good mileage. I drive a Chrysler 300M.

3. What style of house do you prefer? Why?
Ranch, this style is most appealing to me. We are building a four bedroom with four and one half baths using western cedar now.

4. Which television show do you watch most often?
American Idol.

5. Name your favorite sport and tell why you enjoy it above all others.
Softball, basketball and the Arkansas Razorbacks. Go Hogs!

6. Name your favorite athlete.
Michael Jordan.

7. What is your best loved religious hymn? Why?
I have two favorites; *I Know Who Holds Tomorrow* and ***Evening Prayer.* Their messages speak to my heart.**

8. Name the flower you like best. Why is this your favorite?
Red Rose in a bud.

9. Where do you do most of your shopping for clothing?
J. C. Penney and Dollar General.

10. If you were wealthy, where would you like to go on vacation?
To Virginia and Washington D. C. and I would stay in the best hotels.

11. What do you like best about Arkansas?
Its green and the weather changes often.

12. Tell what Alabama means to you.
My grandfather, Odas Seay, and my dad were born there. We visited there one time when I was five or six years old. I was so excited that I stayed awake the entire trip and slept all the time we were there. I could not enjoy meeting the family because I was so sleepy I did not know what I was doing.

13. What technological invention has influenced you most in your lifetime?
Television.

14. How many children do you have?
Three, I have three sons: Bruce Allen; Brently Kell; and Bartley Norman.

15. How do you discipline your children?

Patience and love, seldom did I spank them.

16. What is (was) you career?
Elementary school teacher. I have taught all elementary grades, been an elementary music teacher, a handicapped child teacher, elementary physical education teacher, and resource room coordinator.

17. How do you relieve stress in your life?
Crossword puzzles and other puzzles, and reading.

18. What is the most memorable moment of your life?
When I was three years old, I picked cotton beside my mother. She made me a little cotton sack from a flour sack. She put the baby on her sack. Odas and Margy also worked with her. This is memorable to me because she did not leave us by ourselves, but always kept us close to her.

19. What character traits or attributes of your mother are most prevalent in your personality?
I cry easily like her. She was a kind person and I always try to be kind like she was.

20. Which of your sisters is most like your mother?
I think that I am most like my mother. My brother calls me "Little Thelma."

21. How would you like to be remembered after you die?
That I was a kind, considerate, thoughtful, patient Christian.

22. Tell me about your mother.
She was always working; sewing, cooking, cleaning, and caring for her children. Later she tried to be the best Christian wife she could be when my father suffered from Alzheimer's dementia for ten years before he died.

Thelma provided her children with many life lessons to prepare them to face the challenges of ordinary, as well as certain extraordinary events. She taught her daughters essential facts of life every woman should know to sustain them through psychological challenges. i.e. Thelma lost two infant children in death and was there for Tilda when she lost her first born son.

Legacy
Tilda became a professional teacher.

Chapter 15

Anna Lewis

Third Daughter

Questionnaire

1. Which color do you like best? Do you wear this color often?
Medium to royal blue, yes I do.

2. What model vehicle do you like better than all others? What kind do you drive?
Ford F150 King Cab. I like my truck I am driving now, it is navy blue.

3. What style of house do you prefer? Why?
Victorian, I live in a turn-of-the-century Victorian house now that has a picture of it in the Grant Country Museum in Sheridan, Arkansas.

4. Which television show do you watch most often?
Crime solving and mystery shows.

5. Name your favorite sport and tell why you enjoy it above all others.

Ice skating competitions, it is fascinating to me to see how good they are.

6. Name your favorite athlete.
Kristie Yamaguchi

7. What is your best loved religious hymn? Why?
***Because He Lives,* the words tell me why I am a Christian.**

8. Name the flower you like best. Why is this your favorite?
Petunia, they last so long in the summer and they are so many colors of them.

9. Where do you do most of your shopping for clothing?
Wal Mart or I make them myself. My mother taught me how to sew. I made all of my clothes when I was in high school.

10. If you were wealthy, where would you like to go on vacation?
Hawaii, my oldest grandchild lives in Hawaii. He is ready to graduate from high school.

11. What do you like best about Arkansas?
There are so many different kinds of scenery, mountains, farmland, rivers and lakes.

12. Tell what Alabama means to you.
My father's heritage was in Alabama. We visited there when I was a child. I have many relatives who live there now.

13. What technological invention has influenced you most in your lifetime?
Sewing machine.

14. How many children do you have?
Three: A daughter Angela Irene, and two sons William Lloyd, and David Michael.

15. How do you discipline your children?
In two ways, we spanked them when they were young, and as they got older, we took things away from them and grounded them.

16. What is (was) you career?
A homemaker.

17. How do you relieve stress in your life?
Read the Bible, listen to music, pray and sing.

18. What is the most memorable moment of your life?
I was assigned to make a healthy lunch and demonstrate it to my second grade class. Mom made my lunch and labeled each item as to how good it was for the body. The presentation was supposed to have been in the morning, but it was delayed until the afternoon; so I ate my lunch. Then in the afternoon my presentation consisted of empty jars, an apple core, also I talked about how good the peanut butter and crackers were.

19. What character traits or attributes of your mother are most prevalent in your personality?
Loving the Lord, attending church, making home made bread and sewing.

20. Which of your sisters is most like your mother?
I think that I am, because I am a homemaker and do things like she did.

21. How would you like to be remembered after you die?
I tried to be as good a mother as my Mom was to me.

22. Tell me about your mother.
When I was about twelve years old, I had allergies that gave me blurred vision and I was really scared that I was going to be blind. Mom told me to pray about it. I prayed in tears as my mother told me to "God, I will do anything you want me to do, " and

immediately my eyes cleared. Mom taught me to pray and have faith in God.

Thelma learned to cook, sew, and perform essential household chores to keep the family healthy and wholesome. She always raised a garden, kept chickens, and a dairy cow to add to the family's economy.

Legacy
Anna is an exceptional homemaker.

CHAPTER 16

NANCY GAMMILL

Fourth Daughter

Questionnaire

1. Which color do you like best? Do you wear this color often?
Earth tones... beige and brown, not often.

2. What model vehicle do you like better than all others? What kind do you drive?
Cadillac, I drive a Nisson Murano.

3. What style of house do you prefer? Why?
Victorian with a wrap-around porch. Porches are inviting for fellowship with others.

4. Which television show do you watch most often?
Good, old movies.

5. Name your favorite sport and tell why you enjoy it above all others.
I like to play volleyball and softball, but I like to watch football.

6. Name your favorite athlete.
I do not have a favorite athlete.

7. What is your best loved religious hymn? Why?
***Let Others See Jesus In You*, sometimes people will not read the Bible, but can see Jesus in a life and it changes them.**

8. Name the flower you like best. Why is this your favorite?
American Beauty Rose, the perfect beauty of it.

9. Where do you do most of your shopping for clothing?
Dillard's clearance rack, and other clearance racks. I watch for sales.

10. If you were wealthy, where would you like to go on vacation?
Ireland, it is a lovely green and serene looking country, from the pictures I've seen.

11. What do you like best about Arkansas?
It has a variety of landscapes...mountains, flatland and lots of trees.

12. Tell what Alabama means to you.
Daddy's heritage. We visited there several times when I was growing up. We visited Memorial Day in May. One time we went there in a bob-truck with a tarp on top. I was eight or nine years old at the time.

13. What technological invention has influenced you most in your lifetime?
Microwave

14. How many children do you have?
Three: One daughter, Jonnette, the oldest and two sons, Dustan and Scott.

15. How do you discipline your children?

When they were told to do something, they got a spanking if they did not obey.

16. What is (was) you career?
My career was being a wife and mother, I happened to work at Wal-Mart as a Pharmacist's Technician.

17. How do you relieve stress in your life?
Pray a lot and cry a lot, sometimes I reverse the order.

18. What is the most memorable moment of your life?
When I was six years old, I said little four-letter words because I heard others say them. A kind voice within me gently said, "Don't say those words." From that moment on I could not say those words anymore. Being in church and having wonderful teachers has influenced me to keep these words out of my vocabulary and has kept me focused on the work. I still do not say those words.

19. What character traits or attributes of your mother are most prevalent in your personality?
See to the comfort of others, not self-serving.

20. Which of your sisters is most like your mother?
Anna, she is very industrious like Mother always was. She can make something out of nothing. She has a quiet spoken manner like Mother.

21. How would you like to be remembered after you die?
That I thought of others before I thought of myself. I made myself available to others and the talents that the Lord gave me were exercised. I am not good myself, but God is good and lives in me.

22. Tell me about your mother.
I learned that many times her situation was stressful. I learned not to blame her when she was angry about the circumstances. It took me years to fully understand she only did what she though was right at that time.

Thelma was always willing to help those in need. Although, the Family had limited income, Thelma's ability to provide for the family by gardening, as well as developing egg and milk production became a source of sustenance as well as benevolence. She did not hesitate to extend a helping hand to those in need.

Legacy

Nancy keeps herself involved in church work and community work to aid the needy.

CHAPTER 17

Fifth Daughter

BETTY LOUISE FOSTER

Questionnaire

1. Which color do you like best? Do you wear this color often?
Sky blue, not too often, but I look better in pink.

2. What model vehicle do you like better than all others? What kind do you drive?
Mustang convertible, I drive a Ford Expedition.

3. What style of house do you prefer? Why?
A house that has as many bathrooms as it does bedrooms, so no one has to wait to go to the bathroom.

4. Which television show do you watch most often?
Reality television shows, I stopped watching soap operas years ago.

5. Name your favorite sport and tell why you enjoy it above all others.

Football, when I can play. When I was little all the brothers and sisters played football. I still enjoy watching football games.

6. Name your favorite athlete.
I do not have a favorite.

7. What is your best loved religious hymn? Why?
***Amazing Grace*, this song means a lot to me. I sang it when I was incarcerated on a drug charge. Being arrested was the best thing that ever happened to me. It saved my soul from hell, and the song *Amazing Grace* had a great part in it.**

8. Name the flower you like best. Why is this your favorite?
American Beauty Rose, my father always sang the song to us what one rose would do.

9. Where do you do most of your shopping for clothing?
Wal Mart and yard sales.

10. If you were wealthy, where would you like to go on vacation?
Hawaii, it always has the same season.

11. What do you like best about Arkansas?
The natural beauty in Arkansas is captivating.

12. Tell what Alabama means to you.
My father's childhood home state, I've been there only once.

13. What technological invention has influenced you most in your lifetime?
Dishwasher, I hate washing dishes. When I was little I hid under the table to avoid washing dishes.

14. How many children do you have?
Three: One daughter Erica, and twin sons, Leon and William.

15. How do you discipline your children?

I spanked them. "Spare the rod and spoil the child." Afterwards I always gave them a hug to let them know that they were still loved.

16. What is (was) you career?
Cashier at a gas station.

17. How do you relieve stress in your life?
Usually I do not have much stress, but one time I had a job that was too stressful for me to handle.

18. What is the most memorable moment of your life?
When I was fourteen or fifteen years old, a friend wrote a letter to me. Mom opened it and found out I was smoking cigarettes. That was the only time my mother ever gave me a whipping. I did not smoke again until I became eighteen.

19. What character traits or attributes of your mother are most prevalent in your personality?
I am sensitive like my mother, but I do not have her kind ways.

20. Which of your sisters is most like your mother?
Sheila

21. How would you like to be remembered after you die?
I was and still am the 'comic' of the family. I enjoy making people laugh.

22. Tell me about your mother. **There were so many children growing up that I never had an opportunity to talk with my mother one-on-one. After I grew up, I went to see her and we talked about 'everything.' I treasure those talks today. Those talks are unforgettable.**

Thelma enjoyed life and did whatever she could to help her children be happy, supportive and loving.

Legacy
Betty is a joyous loving mother.
She plans to open a child care center.

CHAPTER 18

SHEILA ANN MULLINS

Sixth Daughter

Questionnaire

1. Which color do you like best? Do you wear this color often?
Purple, No, I do not wear it often, but it was my mother's favorite color.

2. What model vehicle do you like better than all others? What kind do you drive?
I like a Ford Mustang convertible, but I drive a Pontiac Montana van.

3. What style of house do you prefer? Why?
Ranch house with a lakeside view, I do not like stairs and I like beautiful views.

4. Which television show do you watch most often?
The Walton Series

5. Name your favorite sport and tell why you enjoy it above all others.

Baseball, basketball, and boxing, I used to watch those with my father.

6. Name your favorite athlete.
Mohammed Ali

7. What is your best loved religious hymn? Why?
Amazing Grace, the words are so meaningful.

8. Name the flower you like best. Why is this your favorite?
Red rose, they are so pretty.

9. Where do you do most of your shopping for clothing?
Wal-Mart and Dollar General

10. If you were wealthy, where would you like to go on vacation?
Hawaii

11. What do you like best about Arkansas?
The mountains and peaceful scenery.

12. Tell what Alabama means to you.
My family heritage is there, my father was born there; his roots are there.

13. What technological invention has influenced you most in your lifetime?
Camera, I love to take pictures of people and scenery.

14. How many children do you have?
One: Andrew Wesley Mullins.

15. How do you discipline your children?
Spanking and serious talking to; my son has not had a spanking since he was nine or ten years old.

16. What is (was) you career?

Custodian at Newark Elementary School.

17. How do you relieve stress in your life?
Cry and sing country songs.

18. What is the most memorable moment of your life?
When my son, Andrew was born. Mom was in the delivery room with me. As soon as he was born, the doctor put him on my stomach and I said, "Mama doesn't he look like Raymond (my youngest brother)? Mom replied, "Yes he sure does." She was a real comfort during my labor. I was much calmer because of her presence.

19. What character traits or attributes of your mother are most prevalent in your personality?
Her tenderness.

20. Which of your sisters is most like your mother?
Marge.

21. How would you like to be remembered after you die?
As a person everyone liked and loved.

22. Tell me about your mother.
I want to tell you about my mother by talking about the conversation we had when she went to the hospital for her dye test.

After Mom had her test and was put in her room, I volunteered to stay the night with her. After you have one of these tests you have to stay in the hospital and lie still for six hours.

Well, Mom was not getting along with the bed, but she was doing well about keeping still. She told them she would spend the night, but the closer it got to six hours being over, the more she wanted to go home. I was in a chair next to her bed and she told me, " If it is all the same to you, I would rather go home and sleep in my own bed." I told her whatever she wanted to do, if she wanted to go home that was fine.

We told the nurse that Mom had decided to go home. After the six hours were up, I was helping Mom get dressed. I was kneeling down and putting on her socks and shoes. Mom said, "Instead of you going home, after you take me home, you can spend the night with me." I told her I wasn't going anywhere when I took her home, I had planned to stay the night with her. Mom reached down and put her hand on my cheek and said, "You're a good girl!"

The reason I am a good girl comes from how my Mom raised me and the person she was---kind, loving and gentle. Mom was softhearted, also--a trait which I, too have inherited from her. But I am not the only one, as my other siblings have aged, I see those traits in them, more and more. I think I also inherited many of her other traits.

My mother was a remarkable woman!

Thelma was tenderhearted and kind. She always looked for the best in others. She loved to give hugs and seldom put her own needs before someone else's.

Legacy
Sheila is a long-suffering tender hearted 'hugger.'

At Thelma's funeral, her children requested that the minister read I Corinthians, Chapter 13 – commonly called the LOVE CHAPTER. For the children, the reading reflected the character and personal values of their mother. For this virtuous woman, such tribute was perfectly fitting.

"And now abides, FAITH, HOPE, and LOVE – these three; but the greatest of these is love."

CHAPTER 19

LINDA MCGARRAUGH HOPPE

Linda's parents were Scotch Irish. Her father's mother died when he was an infant. Her grandfather raised baby G. (George) C. in Hooker, Arkansas. When he grew up he served in Germany during World War II. The fighting there was so fierce, bloody, and devastating that after he returned home, he wanted never to speak of it. "I don't ever want to see a war fought on USA soil because of what I saw of war in Germany," was the only thing he ever said about it. All of her early childhood, Linda remembers her father as peace-loving, hardworking and a strict disciplinarian.

Her mother, Marie Smelser, was of Scotch-Irish and German descent, and one of thirteen children. She grew up in Beech Grove, Arkansas. Marie had a sparkling and winsome sense of humor; and loved to joke and laugh. She was not a strict disciplinarian, but controlled her children by her wisdom and knowledge of the most persuasive words to say.

Linda was born in Lafe, Arkansas and the oldest of five children. After she graduated as valedictorian of her class, her parents expected her to get a job. Times were hard in that area, the depression still lingered, and parents there did not expect their daughters to go to college immediately after high school graduation as they do now.

She went to work for Southwestern Bell Telephone Company in Jonesboro, Arkansas, as a telephone operator on her eighteenth birthday. After two years there, in 1968, she went to work at First National Bank in Paragould, Arkansas. She started as a switch board operator. When she retired, she was Assistant Vice-President and the Personnel Officer of the bank.

While at the bank, a vibrant and good-looking young man named Ken Hoppe came into the bank on business and saw Linda. When he saw Linda, he liked what he saw. She was, and still is, a most attractive brunette with a beautiful, warm smile. Being an enterprising young man, he asked one of his friends at the bank to introduce him to Linda.

He called her twice and asked to take her to dinner. Both times she had commitments and could not go with him. The third time he called her, he prefaced his invitation by saying, "If you tell me you are busy, I will not call you again." Linda made sure that she was not busy and went with him to dinner. They were married nine months later. After they were married, Linda would tell their friends that she had prayed fervently to God to send the right man into her life. Linda lives by the motto, " Let God Have Control."

After they had been married for several years, Linda came to the realization that she was not going to get pregnant. She and Ken went to a doctor who assisted in placing babies by private adoption. In a few weeks they learned that a "baby boy" had been born in a hospital in a nearby town. They went the next day to get their two day old son.

Words are inadequate to express their joy, fulfillment, and gratitude to God for giving them such a beautiful little boy to be their very own. Now they were a real family. They named him Justin Lynn.

He grew to become an outstanding athlete and set new state records in track. The year he graduated from high school he was named Green County Arkansas' "Outstanding Basketball Player of the Year." During those growing up years their home was pleasantly and constantly full of young people. Linda kept their refrigerator stocked so that those visiting would know that they were greatly welcome.

When not entertaining young people in their home, they were in their car on the road going to attend athletic events in which Justin was involved. Life was wonderful!

After her son's high school graduation, Ken became president of Crowley's Ridge College. Her life is now filled with duties as wife of the president. Although this role takes up much of her time, she still makes time to work in Hillcrest church of Christ's Ladies' Jail Ministry (Both she and Ken are members of this congregation). She teaches women there about Jesus, counsels with them and helps them work through their problems.

Kierstyn Faith, her new granddaughter and only grandchild blessed her life recently. What a beautiful gift from God!

Linda's unassuming serenity impresses anyone who knows her. Her faith in God is radiant. She has a quiet, beautiful spirit that makes this world a more peaceful place in which to live. It is your author's privilege to know her.

CHAPTER 20

LORENE NICHOLS LEATH

Park Nichols, Lorene's father, worked for the Railway Express Company in Searcy, Arkansas. He was a kind and generous man who served as an elder for the Downtown church of Christ in Searcy for many years. Alma, her mother, was devoted to her family and teaching children's Bible classes. She was noted for her annual Easter Egg Hunt conducted in her yard for the church children. She was an expert gardener and landscaped her lawn so beautifully that many couples were married there.

Lorene graduated Harding Academy and enrolled at Harding College. Soon she met a talented young Naval veteran named Boyd Leath. He had been honorably discharged from the Navy and chose to attend Harding College to get his education. Later his and Lorene's generation would be called "The Greatest Generation" because of the valorous and honorable way they conducted themselves during World War II.

Lorene soon decided that she wanted a "MRS" degree more than she wanted a Bachelor's Degree in anything else. They were married in

1951. She went to work at a bank to help Boyd get his degree in music. Her parents furnished them with a tiny apartment.

God blessed them with their first child, Judy, and then He blessed them with another child, Russell and another son, Steve.

Boyd became a school music teacher for a year. Then he decided to work in business instead of in education. However, he used his musical talent to lead congregational singing at various congregations for the next fifty years.

Lorene was a 'stay-at-home-mommy' until her youngest was ready to go to kindergarten. Her children were enrolled in Crowley's Ridge Academy in Paragould, Arkansas. So she worked at the Academy as a secretary in order to help pay the children's tuition. Later she became a bookkeeper and continued to work for Crowley's Ridge Academy for nine years.

Children's Homes, Inc. (sponsored by churches of Christ) was located across the street from the Academy and they needed a bookkeeper and asked Lorene to take the position. She accepted knowing that the pay was low, but she would be helping children.

During the next sixteen years she worked there, the Children's Homes outreach grew and expanded. Their child care operation was donated enough funds, land, and buildings in Kennett, Missouri and North Little Rock, Arkansas, for them to broaden their outreach in those areas. They now have the facilities to see to the needs of over two-hundred children who are not able to live with their parents because they are dead or abusive or for various other reasons.

The program then expanded to include care of unwed mothers care. Lorene kept three unwed mothers into her home until they had their babies. Faithful Christians adopted the babies; gave them their names and good Christian homes.

People who know Lorene tell about her compassionate heart that has comforted many abandoned children and abused children. The children had known such rejection and pain Lorene could not rest until she had done what she could to alleviate their suffering.

Near the end of the war in Viet Nam many orphans were air lifted to the USA from Saigon and placed under the care of Children's Homes Inc. Lorene took many of those home with her on the weekend to give them special attention and love (After she retired, her daughter, Judy went to work for the Children's homes for a few years. Now Judy is a receptionist for Crowley's Ridge College also located in Paragould, Arkansas).

Also, Lorene has worked and supported her husband as an elder's wife. Her husband was an elder over twenty years until his health began to fail and he was no longer able to serve in that capacity.

Those who know Lorene intimately know that she truly has the heart of a servant, never complaining. She helps at every pot-luck, visits the sick, always quiet; never putting herself in the spotlight. Hundreds of children and those she has helped "rise up and call her blessed."

*Note from the author:

Children's Homes, Inc., Crowley's Ridge Academy, and Crowley's Ridge College have enjoyed the leadership of many of God's truly great men, but the day-to-day work of individually helping others could not be done as well as it is done without the love and support of Godly women like Lorene.

Chapter 21

Ellen Dolores Jones Bristoe

Ellen's parents, L.V. and Mayme Jones were farmers, raising cotton, corn, and soybeans. They and their four children lived on an eighty-acre farm in Pascola near Wardell, Missouri. The farm had been repossessed from the previous owners because of the "great depression." After ten years of poor crops, her father sold their farm and bought a small farm in Kentucky. They moved there and raised tobacco.

Ellen enrolled in high school in Lowes, Kentucky. Friends set her up on a "Blind Date" with Morris Bristoe. He was a Kentuckian, whom they all liked. After the date Ellen told her friends, "I didn't like him. I'm not going out with him anymore." Her friends were not at all sympathetic with her. They insisted and kept on insisting until finally she relented and dated Morris again. One and a half years later, on December 28, 1956, when Ellen was eighteen years old, they were married. She was to say later, "Morris is the type of person whom you grow to love and appreciate."

Theirs was a home wedding attended by twenty-five people. They had $20.00 to spend on a wedding trip. They chose to drive to see Hopkinsville, Kentucky and got a motel room. When they went to the restaurant nearby; they were given a free meal because they were newlyweds. Their first baby, Bobby Glenn, was born in Paducah, Kentucky.

Morris took a job with a cable company who transferred him to Rapid City, South Dakota. Their second son, James Michael, was born there.

When Jimmie was three months old, they were planning a trip back to Kentucky to see their families. Jim was sick that morning and was diagnosed with an ear infection. The doctor said it was okay to travel with him, so they headed for home. The baby was very sick with a high fever when they arrived home.

He was placed in the hospital in Paducah, Kentucky as soon as the doctor examined him. Ellen sat with the baby a while and his grandmother came in to relieve her. Ellen was driving to do an errand when she had " A Defining Moment" that changed her life.

Although only twenty-one years old, she was shaken to her very inner being when she realized that she had left 'her baby', who was very ill in the care of someone else. God had given her the baby and she was going to never leave either of her children if they were sick enough to be in the hospital again! She drove back to the hospital and prayed that he would recover. She believes that God answered all of the prayers made for her tiny son because he lived.

Soon thereafter they moved to Bloomington, Indiana. Ellen attended Indiana, University and earned a Hospital Admitting Management Certificate. She worked for Bloomington Hospital until she retired in 1994.

After she and Morris retired in 1994, they began to work for the Indianapolis Speedway during the month of May working security.

They continue to work there for the Indianapolis 500 on Memorial Day, for Nascar races, and Formula One. They also worked for Chicagoland Speedway for two years.

Through the years while living in Bloomington, she was and still is heavily involved in working in North Central church of Christ, their home congregation. She was one of the first women to help coordinate their Ladies' Ministry. She has taught four and five year old Bible classes and assisted in Youth Worship. Now she helps coordinate the Wednesday evening meal before mid-week Bible study and is responsible for helping organize communion preparation. She and Morris coordinated the church's benevolent program for several years.

After the terrible hurricane, Katrina, struck the Gulf Coast, she was one of those who responded by going to Pascagoula, Mississippi working in the church kitchen of Central church of Christ, preparing meals to feed from 40 to 70 workers helping in that area. Since then she and Morris have made another trip in their motor home. Ellen worked in the kitchen and Morris delivered furniture to homes.

"The Defining Moment" that changed her life when Jimmy was ill, grew inside her until now she is not able to leave anyone who needs help until she does something to help them. Ellen is far too modest to make a statement such as this about herself, but your author and friends who know her, know this to be true.

CHAPTER 22

CELIA SOLIS BOON

What an amazing woman! After being a stay-at-home-mom for several years, she resumed her career in her sixties (although she looks as if she were in her late forties). Benton County Cooperative Extension Service, under the aegis of the University of Arkansas, chaired by Robert Seay, needed a person to work in their office to handle their Expanded Food and Nutrition Education Program. They needed a person who had administrative skills, could work well with people and was fluent in Spanish and English. Celia teaches women how to stretch their food dollars, how to shop wisely and how to plan nutritious meals and snacks for their families. When your author visited this office to interview Celia, she saw a large group of families from many cultures. They exuded a confident demeanor that meant, " There is real help here."

Her father Ismael Solis was a barber who owned his own shop in Mercedes, Texas. He was born on a ranch in Mexico, but grew up in Texas in the Rio Grande Valley. An outstanding member of the community, he was loved and admired by all who knew him.

Celia's mother, Julia Ortega, was born in Gallup, New Mexico and was raised in San Diego, California until she was thirteen years old. Then the family moved to Mercedes. Ismael was ten years older than Julia. When they began dating and after they were married, they were admiringly called Robert Taylor and Claudette Colbert because they were so glamorous together. Hollywood stardust shined all around them.

Celia was their second child. When she was six years old, she was enrolled in a Catholic School and remained there until she went to high school. Her mother was insistent that she speak perfect Spanish and perfect English. Neither slang nor idioms were allowed to be spoken in their home. Her mother always told them that they were Americans of Mexican descent. A good scholar, she graduated from high school and ranked fifth in her class of one-hundred-five students.

It was always understood as she was growing up that she would go to college, so she was enrolled at Texas A&I (Arts and Industry) in Kingsville, Texas. She could see the famed King Ranch from her third story dorm room window. Later she moved into an apartment.

Then she decided to move to another apartment. This was a decision that would change her life forever. Because as she was making the move, she met Bill Boon, from Arkansas, who had graduated from the University of Arkansas (Go Hogs!), had finished a two-year tour of duty in the Army, being stationed in Taiwan. He was working in the area and looking for an apartment.

The landlady brought Bill to Celia's apartment to show him the apartment because Celia was moving. It was truly "Love At First Sight." He brought her boxes to use and asked to take her out for a cup of coffee. Both realized that the emotional chemistry between them could not be denied. They were married six months later (When your author interviewed Celia for this story, she said, "I realize that this sounds too syrupy to be true, but that was the way it happened.")

After they were married they moved to Harlingen, Texas where he worked for Kimberly-Clark in sales and she worked as an assistant Home Demonstration Agent for Texas Extension Services. Her job was to teach low-income families how to best use the government commodities that were issued to them (at that time the government did not issue food stamps, but issued food commodities such as rice, beans and grain cereals). Since she was bilingual she taught both Spanish and English speaking women nutritious, but delicious recipes using government issued foods. Her job was her dream come true. She had studied hard at college to earn her degree in Home Economics. Now she was able to use her education to help people.

Two years later she became pregnant with her first child, Julia. As soon as she became pregnant, she resigned from work. At that time it was unheard of for a pregnant women to work in public jobs. Celia became a stay-at-home-mom. They moved to Bentonville, Arkansas because Bill came into the family business. When Julie was six years old, a second daughter, Nancy was born. Celia was happy as a homemaker and mother. When she was sixty she received a call to help in the Cooperative Extension Service in Bentonville. She responded because the need was great and she wanted to help.

Your author asked Celia to tell about one defining moment in her life that would let people know "the real Celia's heart." She said it happened when she was five years old. They lived four miles from the Mexican border and frequently went to Mexico. The land in Mexico was arid and cracked open from the heat. The farmers had no irrigation system. Children her age in the area were beggars seeking for any small something to eat. They were dirty, ragged and shoeless. Celia thought, "Why? Why do I have nice dresses and good shoes? Why is the grass green in Texas? Why do I have a bath often and those children do not? Why do our yards have such beautiful flowers in them? Why are some people so poor and others are so comfortable?" This was the beginnings of what formed her decision to do something to help people. As she grew up, the decision never left her, but solidified and became a reality when she received her college degree. Then she had the proper tools to help others and she did.

CHAPTER 23

MARY STOBAUGH SHAMBARGER

It is my greatest pleasure to introduce these mother-daughter life stories to you. When I was thirty-four years old, married and the mother of four children, I decided that although I had been very successful in business, I wanted to be a teacher. My reason was that teachers make a difference in people's lives and meeting sales quotas only made a difference in my paycheck.

I went to Arkansas State University in nearby Jonesboro, Arkansas, to enroll for the fall semester. They flatly turned me away because I had only completed the ninth grade in high school. Crying all of the way back to Walnut Ridge, I remembered Southern Baptist College just outside of town. In tears, I drove out there. They were friendly, courteous and helpful, and enrolled me for the fall semester in less than thirty minutes. There I made the President's list the first semester, earned the Biology award the second year and graduated with a high GPA. Then the university in Jonesboro accepted me and I earned a bachelors and masters degree there.

My goal of becoming a teacher could only have been realized with the help of dedicated women like Mary Shambarger. They tutored me when I needed it, and were relentless in seeing that I understood the algebra, trigonometry, calculus, and chemistry in order to get a degree in biology.

These few pages are not nearly enough to tell the influence for good that Mary and others like her have done by working for low salaries and faithfully helping others to make the academic grades needed to have desired careers. My gratitude is always overflowing. The name of the college has been changed to Williams' Baptist College (Willodine Hopkins).

Mary's father, Clifford Stobaugh was born and lived near Morrilton, Arkansas. At that time there were many uncut wooded areas there. When he grew up, he became a Timber Broker. He bought and sold tracts of land and timber. Most people in the area knew him and respected him greatly because he was a patient, loving and non-judgmental man.

He married Emma Lee Kissire, also born near Morrilton. Her parents were farmers and landowners. Emma Lee's father wore two hats, farmer and butcher.

During World War II, everyone worked in the war effort. The family and grandfather moved to Wichita, Kansas to work in the Boeing Aircraft plant. After the war ended, they returned to their home in Morrilton and resumed farming.

Emma Lee and Clifford were high school sweethearts who married when Emmalee was just shy of sixteen years old. Clifford was eighteen. They lived with her parents for a while. Mary was their first child. Later they had two more daughters, Martha and Marjorie.

Mary was a highly intelligent child and entered grade school when she was five years old. Because of her unusual academic ability, she was enrolled in Morrilton High School for only three years and graduated when she was sixteen years old.

Her first year at college was spent at Hendrix College in Conway, Arkansas. Then she transferred to Louisiana State University in Baton Rouge. Because she had always loved music, played the piano and sang beautifully, she followed her God-given talents and graduated with a Bachelor's Degree in music and an emphasis in voice.

After college graduation she went to New York City to pursue a musical career. Several auditions later, she got her first job as a professional musician! She sang soprano with the Voices of Walter Shuman.

In a few weeks, she realized that her musical career needed a new direction. She chose to go home and look for work there, rather than change her lifestyle. She loved the LORD enough to drop her dream of becoming famous.

Almost immediately she found a job as a high school voice teacher in Cassville, Missouri. Her dear father, ever mindful of what was best for his daughter, took her to the Baptist church there and spoke with the pastor. "My daughter is moving to Cassville. Her mother and I want her to live in a safe place, preferably with a Christian woman." There was a woman in the congregation who kept women boarders in her home. Mary moved in almost immediately.

During the first semester she met a young athletic coach named Jake Shambarger. By the end of the year they were dating steadily and were married in April of the next year. The year after that their only child, Susan, was born.

In 1960, Jake accepted a position at Southern Baptist College (now Williams Baptist College) in Walnut Ridge, Arkansas. Mary taught there part-time for the first year and the next year she taught full time.

When she began teaching there, there were only twenty-five students in the college choir. By the end of six years the choir had grown to over one hundred. She also directed "The Southern Belles," an ensemble for women and the "Southernaires," an ensemble for men.

During her tenure there, she started the first "Opera Workshop." When she began the workshop there was no stage, no curtains, no theatrical lighting, and no costumes. *(Note from the author...When I interviewed Mary, she was nonchalant about the effort it took to put her first production together. It is your author's opinion that God gave Mary so much talent that she has the capability to be an effective CEO of a large corporation if she had made that choice.)*

The first production, which Mary produced and directed, was *Amahl And The Night Visitors.* She originally planned only one performance, but the public requested additional performances, so she added two more. Every production grew larger and the public attended in larger numbers. Her students knew that Mary invested in their personhood as well as their talents and abilities.

In 1966 she accepted a position at Ouachita Baptist University in Arkadelphia, Arkansas, and taught there for thirty-two years developing many musical ensembles. She directed two choral groups, the "Ouachi-Tones" and the "Ouachita Sounds." These groups made several international cultural exchange trips including:

1971 - USO tour to Panama, Puerto Rico, Cuba,
Islands in the Bahamas and West Indies
1975 - Romania
1977 - Canada, Eastern United States
1979 - Hawaii
1981 - Mexico
1984 - England-Scotland
1986 - Hawaii
1988 - Germany, Austria
1991 - Japan, Korea, China

Her professional activities are many and varied. She has produced and directed live shows for Magic Springs Theme Park in Hot Springs; Kentucky Kingdom in Louisville; and Frontier City in Oklahoma City. Always active in civic organizations, she served as president for the Philharmonic Club, was active in Arkansas Arts Council and Arkansas Governor National Association of Teachers of Singing. She has been a featured soloist in opera, oratorio, and recitals in many states. Always active in church music, she has served as Minister of Music for the First Baptist church in Tuckerman, Piggott, Walnut Ridge, and Arkadelphia churches in Arkansas.

Many well-deserved honors have been awarded to her:
- Elected Coordinator of Voice at OBU
- Appointed Chairman, Applied Music Department at OBU
- Appointed Lena Trimble Goodwin, Endowed Chair
- Arkansas Governor of National Association of Teachers of Singing
- OBU Representative, Arkansas Women in Higher Education

Mary firmly believes that "People can be successful as mathematicians, engineers, or the sciences...but the passion that drives us all is music." The lives of many great scientists including Albert Einstein verify her statement.

Her beloved husband Jake died September 7, 1996. Soon after his death Mary moved to Bentonville, Arkansas to be near her daughter Susan, and son-in-law, Steve, and her grandsons Chad and Jake.

In 1998, Dr. Steve and Susan Goss endowed *Jake Shambarger Faculty Enrichment Fund* and the *Mary Shambarger Competition For Singers* at Ouachita Baptist University. Today Mary's life is full of family, friends, and church activities, but music is still her passion.

Chapter 24

Susan Shambarger Goss

(Daughter of Mary Shambarger, chapter 23)

Susan cannot remember a time when she did not love to sing. Her mother, grandmother, and great-grandmother sang harmony parts and played the piano by ear. Although music was always to be a part of her life, Susan's parents encouraged independent thinking, and instilled in her the belief that "All people are created equal." When Susan was eight years old, she received Jesus Christ as her personal Lord and Savior. Since that time she continues to fall in love with God and His people every day.

Because Susan was a chunky, short little girl, many at school called her "Fatso." In the sixth grade she experienced a growth spurt and became tall and slender to the amazement of her family and schoolmates. She has never forgotten the heartbreak of being called "Fatso." Today every time she sees a child who is overweight or different from other children, she makes it a point, if possible, to say or do something kind for the child.

In high school she starred in both her junior and senior plays, "No, No, Nannette," and "South Pacific." Interest in music was always with her, but she developed a high interest in state and national government. Her teachers chose her to go to Girl's State and while there was elected Attorney General.

After graduating from high school, she entered Ouachita Baptist University. There she met an outstanding young man named, Steve Goss. Her father, who was the university's athletic coach, had recruited Steve to play on the university's basketball team. Both Susan and Steve knew immediately that they wanted to know each other better. He was her first and last date in college. No one else interested either of them.

That fall she enrolled in Ouachita Baptist University. Her major was elementary education with history as her minor. Steve graduated from OBU with a double major, mathematics and chemistry. Steve then enrolled in the University of Arkansas Medical School in Little Rock. The summer after her sophomore year and Steve's junior year, she and Steve were married. Susan says, "Steve is the most compassionate man I have ever met in my life, I love and admire him tremendously."

They waited seven years before they had their first child, Chad. Steve was in his senior year of medical school and Susan was teaching elementary school. After his graduation they had another son, Jake.

When Susan's second son was born, she and Steve named him Scott. As the baby thrived and grew, he looked more and more like Susan's father, Jake. They discussed whether there would be any psychological damage to their baby if they changed his name to Jake. After much discussion and contemplation, it was concluded that there would be no harm done to the baby because he had not learned to respond to his name, just their voice. They began to call the baby Jake. When he was five months old, they went to Little Rock to the Department of Records and officially changed his name. Susan's father wept when they called him and told him why they changed the baby's name.

Steve graduated from medical school with specialties in internal medicine and pediatrics. After many years as a practicing physician, he accepted a position with Mercy Health System in Bentonville, Arkansas. For several years he has been part of their administrative team.

God led Susan to become Women's Ministry Director for the First Baptist Church in Bentonville for six years. She developed a Women's Ministry Team with fourteen team leaders to help the church and community at large..

After many years of lay counseling, God began to show her a need in the area for a Licensed Professional Counselor and a Licensed Marriage and Family Therapist. She resigned her position as Women's Ministry Director of First Baptist Church and enrolled at John Brown University to achieve these goals. She will graduate in December, 2009.

As a Certified Marriage and Family Therapist, she will be able to broaden her scope of helping those in need of personal and spiritual development. Her vision for her future practice is "To instill hope through Christian counseling for individuals, couples, and families."

To meet Susan is a most pleasant experience. Her face shows warmth, love and helpfulness. Her voice exudes strength and confidence. You know immediately that she is a person with Godly understanding of human needs. It was your author's privilege to interview her and to wish her God-speed, when as a woman just over fifty years old; she bravely enters her new career.

CHAPTER 25

DEBORAH (DEB) SUE WILLIAMS KEE

Her father operated a mobile photography studio. He was ahead of his time in family photography because he had a Winnebago outfitted as a studio and drove all over rural Arkansas, Missouri, and Northwest Tennessee where few photographic studios were located. He parked on the parking lot of the largest grocery market in the area and got permission to take and sell photographs. People would line up to get a family picture that was not nearly as expensive as studios charged in large towns and cities in the area.

Her mother was a tiny dark-haired beautiful woman. She had four children, three sons and one daughter (Deb), and worked in the local shoe factory until the family income grew large enough for her to resign. An able homemaker, she was a great cook whose blackberry jam cake became the extended family's favorite at Christmas and other holiday occasions. Deb was always well dressed because her mother lavished her superb sewing skills upon her. Her dresses and leisure wear looked as if they were purchased at expensive boutiques.

Deb was born and grew up in Leachville, Arkansas. She graduated from high school there as an honor student. After graduation she enrolled at Arkansas State University and earned a Bachelor's and Master's degrees in Early Childhood Education. While she was still an undergraduate, she married her high school sweetheart, Dan Kee. They had been dating for three years. Dan is a 6' 6" kind, gentle person with an outgoing personality that makes him everyone's "best friend." Soon after their wedding they moved to Bentonville, Arkansas.

They had two children. Both are young adults and have graduated from college. Their daughter, Kristen, is a project manager for Sam's Club marketing team. Their son, Ryan is married and an interactive web designer for Rockfish Interactive.

Deb's contribution to society is unique. She is relentless in teaching parents, elementary school teachers, and young children caregivers, the importance of quality learning experiences to help develop the young child's intelligence. A member of the educational staff of the Bentonville School System, she provides training locally in the Bentonville area as well as nationally. The State of Arkansas uses her as a consultant to provide early childhood training in Northwest Arkansas. Also, she teaches evening classes at Northwest Ark.com to undergraduates pursuing a degree in Early Childhood Education. Core Knowledge Foundation, Southern Early Childhood Association (SECA), the National Association for the Education of Young Children (NAEYC) use her as a trainer to help those who work with early childhood development. She has traveled the continental United States several times to work with these associations as an expert in her field. The number of young children who have benefited from her selfless and tireless devotion to this cause cannot be counted.

Deb believes that the LORD had a plan for her life. HE wanted her to use her Elementary Administrative Certificate in doing what she is doing. God answered her prayers by bringing her focus and influence from just her classroom into the arena of many, many young children, to help them become physically and mentally whole, with a solid foundation for school and success in society. Her plan for her life had to be changed to fit HIS plan because she had planned to be a school principal.

Deb's experience and successes have made her aware that the most helpful thing any parent can do for his/her child is to read aloud to his/her child daily. This helps develop a loving-nurturing relationship between a parent and child and can make a difference in helping each child to reach its fullest potential. "Every child is worthy of and deserves this!!!"

CHAPTER 26

BRENDA HINES MYERS

Jeremy Myers lives in Cave Springs, Arkansas and is the Associate Minister for the Cave Springs Church of Christ. He works with the young people year round and is instrumental in taking them on mission trips to Honduras every summer. His devotional talks are truly inspirational. Your author has been blessed to hear him speak.

When his parents Rod and Brenda Myers visited Cave Springs Church of Christ, I was introduced to them. After a short conversation, it was apparent that their influence helped Jeremy to be the person he is today. I asked Brenda for an appointment in which I could interview her for her life story. Reading it will inspire you to be more dedicated to Christ as it has also inspired me. (Willodine Hopkins)

Brenda was born to Sarah Dennard and Jimmy Hines in Shreveport, Louisiana at Barksdale Air Force Base where her dad was stationed. Her parents met while in high school at Georgia Christian School near Valdosta, Georgia. After he graduated, her dad spent a year playing ball at Mercer University in Macon, Georgia, and then he joined the Air Force. After boot camp he married his sweetheart, Sarah Dennard. They were seventeen and nineteen years old, respectively. They lived in a tiny trailer and Brenda learned to walk by walking the short distance from the front door to the back door. Later Mack Mahaffey, a Christian they met at church, rented them a house and became a special friend for their family.

An airman's salary would hardly stretch from payday to payday. Once they only had one can of Vienna sausages to eat that day. Brother Shadden, one of the elders came to 'encourage' them after they missed a service. While he was visiting he ate half the can of sausages. They did not miss church services again.

Sarah went to secretarial school and then to work for the telephone company. (The lady that baby sat Brenda during the day later became her mother in law) As soon as they could afford for her to stay home, Sarah became a homemaker, a job at which she excelled.

Brenda's home was always full of people. At different times twenty-two different people stayed in her home for different reasons. Among them was a baby, two boys, unwed mothers, troubled and difficult teens, a girl whose mom died in childbirth and an uncle.

Being exposed to so many people in varied situations gave Brenda different perspectives on walking in other peoples' shoes. It also shaped her beliefs that anyone, despite their backgrounds and the obstacles they face in life can persevere and change the way they proceed through the future. Our past experiences always have an affect on us, but do not have to determine the choices we purposefully make regarding our future. Her dad came from a broken home and alcoholic family and her mom from a broken home, yet they modeled the ability not to become just another statistic.

As a young girl Brenda spent much time in the woods and bayous with her dad who took her hunting and fishing. She learned to bait her own hook at the age of three and could call wild birds. She was a good shot with a 22. She made a deal with her dad that if the animal was only wounded, she got to nurse it back to health and release it--otherwise it was supper. She still likes the outdoors and amuses her students and grandchildren by 'talking' to the birds.

Her dad was an entrepreneur who owned many different businesses -- finance companies, a shopping center, a hardware store, a rendering plant, a fruit market, a vegetable and meat processing plant in Costa Rica. He was also a pilot. All of these different businesses were opportunities to learn new skills and to travel to different places.

Her family moved to Baton Rouge, Louisiana, when she was three, and her father became a lobbyist at the state legislature for the finance industry. He spent much time at the State Capitol Building and he took Brenda with him as much as possible. At an early age, being a precocious child, she became skeptical about politicians because she spent so much time with them in the capitol building.

Once when she was eleven years old, she went with her father to the capitol. He and the senator stepped out into the hall for a few minutes to discuss a matter, leaving Brenda in the senator's seat. The senators were voting on a piece of legislation at the time. When the senator's name was called, the secretary told Brenda to vote for the senator so they could complete the voting. Brenda did not know what to do so she voted "Yes" for the senator; and the secretary continued the roll call. When the senator returned to his seat, Brenda told him what happened. He was pleased she had voted the way he would have.

As the family grew more financially successful they desired to give their children a quality Christian education. In her ninth grade year Brenda attended Georgia Christian High School, where she met Rodney "Rod" Claude Myers, her future husband.

During high school Brenda and Rod dated other people, though Rod was interested in Brenda. It was not until college years that they both became interested in one other. He being a persistent kind of guy, managed to sit by her when the school went on chorus trips. He would play his guitar and sing to her. After they went to Europe on a school chorus trip, Brenda began to be impressed with his day-to-day dedication to Christ. He was truly a dedicated Christian and never faltered.

Both enrolled in Harding University in Searcy, Arkansas. Brenda received her Bachelor's Degree in Early Childhood Education and Elementary Education. They were married at the end of their junior year. Soon after graduation, they moved to Memphis in order for Rod to enroll in Harding Graduate School of Religion. There he earned a degree in Christian Apologetics.

They were part of a missions team who moved to Norfolk, Virginia to teach the Gospel there. They lived there for two years and their first baby, a daughter, Rachel was born. Then their financial support stopped.

Rod became the located preacher for the Church of Christ in Pompano Beach, Florida. They lived there for two and one half-years. Their son, Jeremy was born there. Their next stop was Homestead, Florida where Rod served as Principal/Administrator of Redland Christian Academy for two years. They felt it was a way to give back to others who had invested time in their Christian education. Dustin was born while they lived there. God blessed them in helping them sell their home to clear the way for their next move.

Then they moved to Boca Raton, Florida. Their son Joshua was born there. Two years later their son, Timothy blessed their life. Rod preached for the Church of Christ in Delray Beach for ten years. They loved the Christians and the work in Delray, but feared that the abundance of money and affluent community lifestyles would influence their children adversely. Classmates being picked up by limos and having lots of money was out of line with preacher's salary.

The Central Church of Christ in Sarasota, Florida asked them to move there. The Myers family has been in Sarasota for almost seventeen years. They love the Christians and the work there. Brenda has been teaching in the public school system for fifteen years, mainly as a kindergarten teacher.

Brenda and Rod now have four grandchildren, one grand- daughter, three grandsons, and another grandson on the way. Now that her children are married and have children of their own, they relish reading what they have named "The Funny Book." As her children were growing up, Brenda recorded many of the things her children said and did when they were little. She continues to do this for her grandchildren. She tells them part of her job is remembering.

When your author asked Brenda to describe an event that affected her and defined her personality, she did not hesitate to answer that it was when her four year old brother, Danny was killed in an accident. She was nine years old at the time and her brother Doug was seven. Her family was greatly affected by the sorrow they all felt from the loss of her brother. Having experienced that sorrow made her a better person.

Brenda believes that God always gives Christians what is needed. Her mother had her tubes tied after Danny's birth. Almost miraculously, three years after Danny's death, her mother became pregnant and gave birth to her brother, Tim. This brother was regarded as a true gift from God to ease their sorrow. Tim was in the first Cradle Roll Class Brenda taught. She continued to teach Cradle Roll for the next forty years.

Brenda loves music, singing, playing the piano and guitar with her husband and sons. She likes cooking and having others over for meals. No matter how many demands for Brenda's attention, she always has a loving and willing ear for any friend in need. She has been a speaker for Ladies' Days and led singing for Ladies' Days and Retreats.

The last two years have been full of changes for Brenda and her family. She was severely injured by a child at school. After a visit to Mayo Clinic, diagnosis of her many problems was finally fully discovered and reported. Treatment has begun to repair a torn meniscus in her knee, a torn rotator cuff, carpel tunnel, and treatment for rheumatoid arthritis and some neurological tissues. With the support of her family and friends and faith, the future will be better. Her husband is a constant source of encouragement and help to her during these times and she is grateful he cares for her so gently.

Compassion is a key characteristic in Brenda's personality. Once when she was taking her children home from a dental appointment, they saw a poor disheveled man sitting on the side of the road.

"Look at that bum!" one of the children said.
Brenda looked at him and told her children.
"Look at his foot, it is swollen and hurts.
Doesn't he look hungry to you?"
The children all nodded and said,
"Yes, he looks hungry.
What can we do to help him? "
Brenda said, "I have about five dollars in my purse.
I was going to take you all to Mc Donald's for French Fries,
Would you like to buy the man a hamburger and drink instead?"
The children had been taught to be truly unselfish.
They all agreed to not get the French fries,
they all wanted to feed the poor man.
When they gave him the food,
He looked at them and said,
"God Bless You!"

The children loved their mother for helping them to be a blessing to a poor person. Any one who knows Brenda realizes that she is indeed blessed by the LORD and that she in turn blesses all that she meets.

CHAPTER 27

GEORGIA FAYE HOWELL COOK

Her father was Ernest Howell. He was a leader-of-men, but always kind-spoken and wise. He farmed cotton and grain and raised cattle. His outgoing personality helped him to make friends easily. He was a devout Christian and later served as an elder in the local church of Christ.

In those days everyone went to town on Saturday afternoon and stayed until nearly bedtime. Farmers, who labored long and hard in the fields, quit at noon, bathed in a washtub and took their wives and children, who had also bathed and dressed in near-best clothes, to town.

Bulo, Oklahoma was not far from Reydon, and this particular Saturday, Ernest decided to go to Bulo. He was twenty-five years old at the time. Someone introduced him to a pretty, petite, dark-haired young woman named, Hazel Juanita Copenhaver. She was from a large family. When he saw her he was immediately attracted to her, but because she was so shy and reserved, he had to take the lead in getting acquainted with her.

After a short courtship, they were married on December 8, 1935. Ernest made arrangements to buy the Mark Terry homestead in Bulo. It was one-hundred-sixty acres and had a four-room house and a barn on it.

When Hazel became pregnant, she was never aware that she was carrying twins. Hers was a very difficult labor, then she gave birth to a son, who was named Rollie Ray. She suffered another long and agonizing four hours before her daughter, Georgia Faye was born. After the twins were born, the doctor was most emphatic in stressing that Hazel was never to try to have another baby. She would most certainly die if she tried.

How the family rejoiced after the twins were born! What made their birth so extra special was that they had been born on Hazel's twin sister's, Leta's and Cleta's birthday, April first. The young aunts immediately made the sweet babies their projects to care for. They rocked, walked, and played with them continually.

The Great Depression held a tight grip on this country and times were indeed hard for young parents. Hazel had only one dozen diapers for her babies. This means that she had to wash at least twice a day. She pumped water and scrubbed diapers on a rub-board until they were able to buy additional diapers. Georgia Faye and Rollie Ray thrived under the loving care of their parents, young aunts, and grandparents.

Georgia Faye's earliest memory is walking to the three-room school holding her brother's hand. She did not realize at the time, that she would never let go of his hand. Even after she married, she lived close to her twin brother.

Georgia Faye was taught about her Savior all of her life. She became a Christian at twelve years old. When she was seventeen years old she and her cousin, Alma Myers, taught a kindergarten Sunday School class in their home congregation.

One Valentine's Day, Georgia Faye and Alma were determined that each of their young students were going to get a valentine from their Sunday School teachers (valentines could be bought then for one cent each). With almost a dollar between them, they walked twelve miles to Sayre, Oklahoma, to buy valentines.

After buying the valentines, they stopped at a Champion gas station to rest a little before the long twelve mile walk back home. Georgia Faye was pretty, slender, blonde, with true-blue eyes, and naturally curly hair. It is no wonder that Calvin Cook, an industrious young man who worked at the gas station, would take notice of Georgia Faye. Her winning smile and out-going personality help her make friends easily still today.

Calvin did not want or try to resist her smile. He owned a slick-shinny 1949 2-door Ford, his pride and joy. He offered to take both girls to Bulo. Since there were two girls, they decided it was safe to let him take them. After all it was a long twelve mile walk and they had already walked twelve miles that day! They charmingly accepted his offer.

As Calvin was driving west to Bulo, a man who was drunk U-turned in front of them and stopped. Calvin could not avoid hitting him head-on. They were not seriously hurt, Georgia Faye hit her head on the dash board giving her forehead a deep bruise and two enormous black eyes. Calvin's car was demolished. A school bus picked up the girls and took them home. Calvin got a wrecker to tow his car back to the station where he worked.

As usual, Georgia Faye's parents went to Sayre the next Saturday. Georgia Faye walked to the gas station where Calvin worked to "check on how much progress Calvin had made on repairing his car."

Calvin began to call on her when he got off work. He worked sixteen hours a day six days a week and part of Sunday. He would stop by her house twice a week after he got off work at 10 P.M., drive the twelve miles to her house to see her.

They sat on the front porch steps or inside his car if the weather was cool until Georgia Faye's mother would flip the front porch light off for a few seconds and then turn it back on. This was the signal for Georgia Faye to say, "Goodnight" and come inside her house.

On November 1, 1957, they were married at the Bulo, Oklahoma church of Christ. They had no money for a honeymoon; Calvin had to go to work the next day. Georgia Faye's grandfather owned a tiny rent house in Sayre. They paid him twenty-five dollars a month rent. Calvin made thirty dollars a week. They managed to stay inside their budget and be independent. They were very happy!

Eleven months later their first child, a daughter who was named Janice Faye was born. Five years after that their second daughter, Darla Jean was born. Before her birth they had managed to buy a new house and had moved into it.

In 1983 tragedy struck the family. Georgia Faye's twin brother was in a terrible automobile accident that broke his neck and paralyzed him from his chest down. He could use his arms, but had no control over his legs, bowels or urine.

He had married a sweet, caring young woman named Glora Dawn Thompson and they had two small children. At first he was expected to die from his injuries. Georgia Faye stayed six weeks in the hospital at his bedside. She never went home to rest. Calvin and her mother took care of her children. Later he was transferred to Amarillo to a rehab hospital, then on to Denver to another rehab hospital.

Georgia Faye told your author of her great admiration and love for her sister-in-law, Glora. Glora and the family tenderly and unselfishly cared for Rollie Ray for the next eighteen years. His children grew up knowing that they had a family that would never let them down. Georgia Faye and Calvin altered their lifestyle to spend more time with Rollie Ray and his family. Their devotion has been an example for every family who has a disabled person in it. Rollie Ray died in 2002. Georgia Faye still misses her twin brother.

After her young daughters went to school Georgia Faye began to be a career woman. She trained as an abstractor and worked for Beckham County Abstract Company for five years. Then she began working for Allison Enterprises, an oil and gas production company. Her responsibility was to check records at various courthouses to get the requirements for mineral buying and leasing. In the early 1990's the company went out of business.

When her daughter Janice began to operate "Apple Dumpling Pre-School" in Sayre, Georgia Faye put on another hat. She began working with three and four year olds in the school.

Her dear father died in 1974 and her mother never remarried. As her mother grew older and could no longer care for herself, Calvin and Georgia Faye moved in the house with her. Both she and Calvin were retired. She spoke to your author in glowing terms praising her husband's unselfish attitude and willing hands helping her care for her mother. Grievous health problems plagued her mother in old age. Georgia Faye and Calvin stayed with her for six years.

Today Georgia Faye says that those years were some of the sweetest years of her life. She treasures the time spent with her mother. She learned the real quality person that her mother was. Time will never erase the preciousness of those times.

Today Georgia Faye and Calvin live in Bentonville, Arkansas. They are active members of the Cave Springs church of Christ. They continue to work in the church and stay busy helping people. They are a blessing to all who know them. It was your author's privilege to be their neighbor and to write this account of Georgia Faye's life.

CHAPTER 28

TSERENPEL TSENDJA

Tserenpel visited me in my home for the Christmas holidays in 2008. She came with her sister, Tserenchunt Legden and her family. Tserenchunt and I are dear friends and it was my pleasure to have her sister in my home. Tserenpel does not speak English, so Tserenchunt acted as our interpreter. Tserenpel's story is completely compelling. I was enthralled from the moment she began to tell it. You will be inspired by the drama of her childhood and her dedication to her patients (Willodine Hopkins).

Her father, Legden Delegbal was born in 1923 in Mongolia. For many generations his family wore the title "Taij," a title traditionally given to the descendants of Genghis Kahn. Her grandfather and great-grandfather had that title, but in 1921 when the People's Revolution came into power, the title could not be used because communism declares everyone to be equal (the title, Taij, implies a person who is superior in rank to others). After the Democratic Revolution in 1990, the title Taij was not restored, but the clan name "Borjigon" was restored. Her father was a herdsman as were his parents and grandparents before him.

Her mother's name was Dejidbum. She was orphaned at an early age, and later saddened by the deaths of her younger brothers at ages seven and nine because of complications from having measles (During the 30's and 40's many children died from measles and chickenpox). An uncle, a very wise and intelligent man, took care of Dejidbum. The communists arrested him during the purge in 1937, and shot him to death, creating more tragedy in her life.

Her mother also, was of herdsman heritage. She would sing lyric melody to the sheep and goats. Sometimes a mother animal would reject her baby. Dejidbum would pull the mother-sheep or mother-goat close to her newborn and sing in the moonlight "Toig, toig" to the sheep and "Tsiig, tsiig" to the goats. The song softened and touched the feelings of the animal's mother. The first acceptance of the babies brought real tears to the eyes of the accepting mother, and then she would bleat and smell her newborn baby.

Her parents married when both were barely nineteen years old. After their first child was born and they were both still nineteen, there was fierce fighting on the eastern side of Mongolia, near the China border. All of the men in the area were conscripted to defend Mongolia against the Japanese. Legden rode to the battle on a horse. He was anxious to defend his country and rode so urgently that he fell from the horse and severely crushed his collarbone. It took five days and nights to transport him to the hospital in Ulaanbaatar (capital of Mongolia). Because of the war, it was five years before he was able to return home. He was a true WWII hero.

After he returned home a second daughter was born. When she was two years old a third daughter, Tserenpel, was born. She was an unusually beautiful baby girl.

When she was four and a half months old, a famous man, Tavkhai, came to visit in their home. He was an expert horse-trainer and possessed an extraordinary singing voice. Most of his fame was the magnificent way he sang Mongolian "long-song" (a specific genre of music) in such a memorably beautiful style. One had to have unique singing talent given to very few to sing native Mongolian "long song." He must be able to sing and sustain high notes for a very long time (somewhat similar to a superb grand operatic tenor).

Tavkhai saw beautiful Tserenpel and told her parents, " I will adopt your child." He was married and had four children, one adopted and three his natural children.

Two weeks later, when Tserenpel became five months old, Tavkhai returned to her home and placed the required symbolic blue silk scarf upon the family altar. (This same ceremony is performed when a marriage is arranged. The father of the groom places a blue silk scarf upon the family altar signifying that he accepts this girl into his family and will provide for all of her needs.) This signified legally that he took beautiful Tserenpel into his family as his own child.

Shortly after Tserenpel was adopted Tavkhaii fell in love with a much younger woman and left his wife and five children. Tsendjav, the first wife continued to give loving care to Tserenpel and her other children.

As a young child, Tserenpel helped to herd the sheep. When she became eight years old, her adoptive mother took her to meet her birth parents. They exchanged gifts and maintained a good relationship until both parents died.

Tserenpel never felt that her parents gave her away to be adopted. It was the custom of their people to do such things. She is honored today for her parents' lineage that is held in high esteem by all. Her adoptive mother committed her life and love to Tserenpel. They have shared fully in her life, the happy times and when times were not so good. Her adoptive sister Tarzadmaa and adoptive brothers Chimeddorj, Myahandorji, and Dashdavaa; as well as her favorite nephew Zorigbaatar are as dear to her heart as her genetic siblings.

She entered elementary school at age nine, then on to high school and then on to medical school. Her future husband, Otgonbaatar, entered the same university. She helped him with his studies and they became close friends.

At that time Mongolian students used to go to state farms to help the farmers with the fall harvest for six weeks. They worked together in the same harvest and became closer friends. When they were apart they missed each other terribly. They knew that they were really deeply in love, but Tserenpel wanted to wait until she graduated for them to marry, but love conquered. They decided to marry before graduation. Their friends encouraged them to go ahead because they were such an ideal couple.

The next year she bore a son, whom they named Turbold and then two more sons, named Turbat and Turmoenkh. In Mongolia when a woman bears three sons, she is honored as a good daughter-in-law. She is called "darhan ber."

She graduated from the Mongolian Medical University in 1975. Her husband also became a doctor. He specialized in public hygiene and Tserenpel specialized in cardiology. She says her life was happy because she always wanted to be a doctor and she had fulfilled that dream.

Tserenpel has been working in the First Hospital of Ulaanbaatar for ten years. Her patients honor her for her professionalism and good character. Her life is fulfilled because she knows that she helps heal those suffering from sickness and diseases. To "treat everyone in a good and graceful way, not depending upon his or her attitude towards me," is a guiding principal Tserenpel lives by.

In 2006, after she had worked as a cardiologist for thirty-three years, a team of American doctors came to the hospital in which Tserenpel worked. When they saw that the hospital did not have modern equipment to treat heart patients, they took action and contacted a charitable foundation in America and persuaded them to buy modern technological heart-care equipment for the hospital. Then two doctors, a husband and wife team, came to her cardiology department and arranged for her to come to Baton Rouge, Louisiana for six weeks to learn how to operate the new equipment.

When asked about her goals for the future, she responded: "My short term goal is to improve the cardiology department in the hospital in which I work and my long term goal is to build a new modern hospital furnished with the latest technological equipment in which to help save the lives of my beloved people."

CHAPTER 29

RUBY LOUISE SHAVER WILSON

Ruby's father's name was Luther Freeman Shaver and he was called L.F. During the extreme hard times of the Great Depression, he was a cotton and corn farmer in the hills of Northeast Arkansas, in the Palestine Community. Although he was too poor to own horses and a wagon, his faith in God remained steadfast. He walked ahead of his family leading them to church services anytime there was a meeting of the church. If it was a night service, he lit a lantern, held it high above his head and walked ahead of them to the service. If there was snow and ice on the ground, he still held the lantern high and led his family to worship God. Blessed with a powerful melodious bass voice, he sang vigorously whatever the song. Even if the song had a bass lead, he did not hesitate to sing the lead.

The church met in a one-room-meeting-house. Sunday School class for the adults was conducted in the front of the building. All of the children aged three to ten were taught the Bible by a sweet voiced, Christian woman. No child ever misbehaved because its parents were sitting in the front and would take immediate action if their child caused the slightest problem. Because their home and church environments were spiritual and Bible oriented, the children became Christians at an early age and avid Bible scholars as well.

Ruby's mother's name was Dora Bell. She loved her children unselfishly and carefully washed "Mother's Best" flour sacks on the washboard until the advertising was washed away. She sewed almost everything that her family wore. Since they were too poor to buy elastic, she made her daughter's underpants with flour sacks and made a drawstring and a button, ensuring that her daughter's had no embarrassing moments with their underpants. Later when the girls were older, she cut strips from a worn out tire inner tube to make garters to hold up their stockings.

Her son, Ray, was also blessed by his mother's sewing ability. He was dressed in beautifully fashioned 'flour sack' shirts and little britches tailored in such exquisite fashion; they would sell for many, many dollars on today's market.

Every morning before daylight Dora "B" built a fire in her wood stove in the kitchen. She made delicious biscuits for breakfast that would be the envy of gourmet cooks today. Her fried fruit pies were truly memorable.

L. F. was the Bible scholar in the family. No matter how long the day's work, after supper the family gathered around the kitchen table for a family devotional. Although he was a strict disciplinarian, there was Godly kindness in his discipline. The Bible was read aloud and he carefully explained the deeper meanings to his children. The children all knew that he had taught their mother about Jesus and had baptized her into Christ.

Ruby was educated in a large one-room schoolhouse. An excellent teacher, named Mildred Carroll, taught grades one through eight. By the time a student finished the eighth grade there, he/she knew almost everything a student was required to know in grades one through eight; because daily each reviewed lower grades each had been through and were introduced to upper grade knowledge early; preparing them to be grade-ready when entering a higher grade. If a young student had any problem, an older student took the younger one aside and tutored the younger one until he/she became competent and was able to work at grade level.

Every Friday afternoon the teacher conducted a "Ciphering Contest." Students from other schools would attend and participate. A young student named, Cecil Wilson, from the Brakebill Community, attended almost every Friday. He was good in math, but not as good as Ruby's sister Livla because Livla won almost every Friday. Cecil was three years older than Ruby and he liked Ruby. Ruby was impressed with Cecil, but she was too young to date anyone.

Every summer Palestine church of Christ had a two-week Gospel meeting. People came from all around. The churchyard was full to overflowing with horses and wagons. There was no electricity (no one had electricity in the area), only two Aladdin lamps. Cecil's family attended every night. Ruby would sit by an open window. Before Cecil would enter the building, he would go quietly up to the window and whisper to Ruby asking her for a date after the meeting was over. This went on for two years.

Everyone in the area loved music. Families took turns hosting 'Musical Evenings" in their home. Cecil played the violin and guitar. He was a talented musician. Ruby attended these events with her parents. By the time Ruby was fifteen and Cecil was eighteen, he had already asked Ruby to marry him.

There were no employment opportunities in Northeast Arkansas during the 1930's, but Cecil heard that there were job openings in St. Louis. He decided to leave home and go to St. Louis and get a job. He confided to Ruby that he was leaving to go to work in St. Louis. Ruby became tearful and greatly emotional. She cried to Cecil, "If you go, you won't come back!" He assured her that when he had money he would come back to her and marry her.

Ruby believed she had come to a pivotal moment in her life. She quickly decided what action was best for her to take. Through her tears, she said, "Let's talk to my parents and see if they will give their permission for us to marry now?" Her parents gave their permission and they were married in a beautiful home-wedding setting in her parents' living room on June 6, 1937.

They lived in the house with Cecil's parents through harvest time in the fall, picked cotton and saved their money. Cecil went to St. Louis and got a job as a dishwasher in a hotel restaurant. He rented a small one-room apartment so he and Ruby could be together. The apartment cost $3.00 per week and Cecil made $17.50 per week. They lived frugally and saved money. As soon as Ruby turned sixteen she got a job at Barnes Hospital in the dining room. They moved to a larger apartment.

By the time their first child, a son whom they named Donald Ray, was born, they had moved up into a three-bedroom apartment.

Cecil was awarded a scholarship to attend the School of Horology at Poplar Bluff, Missouri. Their second Michael Lewis was born there. When not attending classes he worked in a jewelry store. Ruby as a "stay-at-home-mommy" was extremely careful with the household expenses. They began saving money to buy their own jewelry store.

They sold their car, banked the money, and Ruby rode the bus to the grocery market. They also rode the bus to church. It is easy to see in one's imagination a young mother with two active little boys, struggling with paper grocery sacks, boarding a bus and keeping the little ones still and in their seats while holding on to her purse and two heavy grocery sacks that contained a week's supply of food. Then getting off the bus, and watching the boys carefully to keep them out of the busy streets, while carrying the sacks and walking the way back to her apartment. With hope in her heart Ruby walked home, she was looking toward their future!

In 1947 they moved to Pocahontas, Arkansas. The owner of the local drug store, Mr. Perrin, moved everything to one side of the store and Cecil set up a jewelry store on the other side, paying the owner a commission on everything he sold.

Ruby continued to run a thrifty household saving every penny she could from the household expenses. It two years, they bought their own store. Then God blessed them with a baby daughter, whom they named Sheila. Their business flourished and they bought their own home.

The house that they bought was on three acres. Don and Mike created a ball field on their property and the neighborhood children played ball on it every minute that their parents would permit them to do so. Ruby made cupcakes and Kool-Aid for refreshments. Don hit so many home runs that he was nicknamed "Homer," a nickname he is lovingly called by many family members and friends today.

Their home was near the high school. On rainy days the neighborhood children went inside the school gym and played basketball. In the Bible Belt during the times of the 'Depression" and for several years thereafter, nobody locked doors on their homes, the school building, or the church buildings. Thievery was a really rare occurrence.

Besides being an outstanding businessman, Cecil was a natural orator. He preached for nearly every church in Northeast Arkansas. His Bible knowledge was great and his preaching ability was noteworthy. Ruby accompanied him everywhere and learned to love the people and they learned to love her.

Her son Mike, became a Gospel preacher wrote a church history book titled "Arkansas Christians," which is a standard in Christian's home libraries in Arkansas today, as well as on Arkansas preacher's library shelves.

Her life was tragically changed when Cecil died suddenly of a major heart attack in 1984. She grieved deeply for a long time. Then she knew that she was facing a new lifestyle as a widow. She bought a car and learned to drive. Her family and friends were amazed at her tenacity. She continued to live in Pocahontas and stay active in church work.

Some friends in Bono, Arkansas started a "Musical Evening" every Friday night. Any musician who wished to could come and play and any who wanted to just sit and listen were invited to do so for a small fee. The listening attendance and musician participation grew rapidly and the "Musical Evening" became a popular area-wide institution. Ruby enjoyed the evenings immensely because they reminded her of her early childhood.

Ruby was to suffer inconsolable grief again when her son, Mike, died in a boating accident in 2002. Her family and Christian friends gathered around her doing all that they could to help her with such a loss. They still continue to surround her with love and practical help.

Today, Ruby is nearing ninety years old. She attends every church service except when health problems prevent her. She is an inspiration to all. Her influence is alive and active. She considers herself blessed because one grandson is a full-time Gospel preacher and her granddaughters and their husbands all are active Christians. The seeds sown when she was young and in good health are now reaping a of harvest of joy.

About The Authors

Nita Brinkley Smith was married to Arlin Brinkley and has five sons. After her sons became adults, she began a new career working in the Crowley's Ridge College bookstore. When her husband Arlin died, she continued to work there.

Five years after Arlin's death she married Emmett Smith, founder of Crowley's Ridge Academy and Crowley's Ridge College. They led one of the mission teams to Communist Romania after the revolution there. Phone headquarters for the campaign was in their apartment. After a two-month campaign, where everyone on the team taught the Bible day and night, over one-hundred people were baptized into Christ.

Eight months later, the team returned to Romania. This second campaign resulted in over three-hundred being baptized into Christ, thus making the Church of Christ there one of the largest congregations of the Church of Christ in Europe.

After the breakup of the U.S.S.R., Ukraine declared its independence from that nation. Harding University planned a mission trip to the Ukraine and asked Emmett and Nita to go with them to Donetsk. Over one-hundred Christians went on this effort.

There they helped establish ten congregations of the Church of Christ. Not speaking the language, they worked using interpreters and many of the interpreters were their first converts.

Nita taught a large group of women what Christian women need to know about birth control methods that are God approved, submission to their husbands, and how to teach their own children about Jesus and HIS church.

Emmett died shortly after they returned home. As a widow, Nita works diligently teaching people through World Bible School and sending Bible literature to people in prison. She is an inspiration to all privileged to know her.

Willodine Hopkins, a widow with four grown children, was born and lived many years of her life in Northeast Arkansas. She holds a Bachelor's Degree and a Master's Degree in Biology in Education from Arkansas State University. While living in Arkansas, she taught in the Clover Bend and Tuckerman public school districts several years. She then made a career change and began to teach in Christian educational institutions, Crowley's Ridge Academy for two years, Crowley's Ridge College for five years.

While on the faculty of Crowley's Ridge College, she was the Woman's Coordinator for their Comprehensive Evangelism Program, organizing and sending "Campaigns for Christ" groups to New England, Panama, Canada and China. On weekends she organized and conducted nearly one-hundred "1,000 for Christ" Ladies' Rallies. In each rally, a thousand persons were taught the Gospel using Bible correspondence courses. She also coordinated "Target-A-Nation" evangelism workshops in which missionaries, campaign workers and interested Christians assembled to learn the peoples and cultures of the nations and how to plan to reach each nation with the Gospel.

She then relocated to Southern California, continued her education by taking courses from California State University and the University of California at various campuses in the evening and on Saturdays, while she taught in Normandie Christian School in Los Angeles and later for Los Angeles Unified School District. When she retired from teaching, she pursued her dream of becoming a writer.

Also, after her retirement she became heavily involved in Friendspeak, a part of Let's Start Talking program, teaching the Gospel to international students using Friendspeak materials. She taught students from China, South Korea, Mongolia, Turkey, and Thailand.

As a teacher of Biblical women and women's role in evangelism, she has taught at Retreats, Special Luncheons, Creative Writing Seminars, and Soul Winning Workshops at Crowley's Ridge College, Biola University, Pepperdine University, and was the Keynote speaker at various women's conventions and conferences in many U.S. states and Canada.

PUBLISHED WORKS:

CHRONOLOGICALLY

Author uses her maiden name, Willodine Hopkins

Once a month articles: *The Way of Truth*, a periodical published in Rampachodavaram, India (1982-1983)

Article: Church Growth, The *Most Successful Teacher About Jesus: A Pattern For Soul Winning,* (4th Quarter, 2004)

Growing Up Noiskleta, a poem booklet of Cherokee Folklore, Private publication (2004)

Article: *Christian Woman* magazine, *Evangelizing the World At Home* (November-December 2007)

Books:

A History of the Influence of Women, (5-4-2004)

Learning to Integrate the Attributes of God Into Our Own Personality

Volume I, (2-21-2005)

In His Presence My Heart is Made Strong, (12-7-2005)

Learning To Integrate The Attributes Of God Into Our Own Personality Volume II, (2-7-2007)

The Valiant Christian Woman, Volume I, with Mary Ulmet (3-15, 2007).

Solomon's Legacy for Women (1-23-2008)

Women's Voices In The Church Today, with Rynn Cooper (7-22- 2008).

Significant Women In the Signs Of God (January 2010)

Work in progress - Book

God's Gift To Women: The Glory Of The Scarlet Thread (Available 1-2011)

LaVergne, TN USA
08 March 2010
175185LV00003B/4/P

9 781449 070953